THE WITCH'S APPRENTICE

Little
MAGIC

RITUALS

Océane Laïssouk is an amulet maker, illustrator and practitioner of Japanese medicine. She draws from her heritage, mixing her French roots with Berber origins, and is devoted to magic grounded in everyday life. Her Instagram page is @almatribal_therapie

Estelle Modot is an alchemist, herbalist and botanist. Passionate about the dream world, Estelle works in understanding its subtleties, and shares these philosophies on her Instagram, @lespotionsdelitha

Petits Rituels de Magie first published in 2021 by Larousse
This English hardback edition published in 2022 by Quadrille

First published in 2022 by Quadrille,
an imprint of Hardie Grant Publishing
52–54 Southwark Street
London SE1 1UN
quadrille.com

TEXT Océane Laïssouk and Estelle Modot
ART DIRECTION Géraldine Lamy
DESIGN Valentine Antenni

For the English language hardback edition:
MANAGING DIRECTOR Sarah Lavelle
COMMISSIONING EDITOR Sarah Thickett
DESIGNER Alicia House
HEAD OF PRODUCTION Stephen Lang
PRODUCTION CONTROLLER Sabeena Atchia

Cataloguing in Publication Data: a catalogue record for this book is available from the British Library.

Text © Larousse 2021
Layout © Quadrille 2022

ISBN 978 1 78713 930 5
Printed in China

MIX
Paper from
responsible so___
FSC™ C020___

Océane Laïssouk
Estelle Modot

THE WITCH'S  APPRENTICE

Little
MAGIC
RITUALS

The essential witch's kit for reconnecting
with yourself and with nature

Hardie Grant

QUADRILLE

Contents

The WORLD of Wiccans

Wiccan philosophy & principles

A brief history of Wicca

Wiccan philosophy can be summed up in a single sentence: "Do what you will, so long as it harms none." Wiccans live according to the principles of tolerance and respect for nature, existing in harmony with their environment and with others, in a spirit of sharing, mutual support and love.

White magic

Magic is a practice based on the belief that we can influence events and natural forces in the material world through rituals using supernatural powers. Magical beliefs were a central part of tribal societies for centuries, but the emergence of monotheistic religions and the growth of scientific knowledge saw a move away from traditional magical practices.

There are two magical opposites: goetia, a form of dark magic, and theurgy, a lighter magic. It was during the Middle Ages that colour distinctions between forms of magic emerged. Black magic, white magic, red magic and green magic, to name but a few, came into being. White magic is the "purest" because it is derived from love and benevolence.

Wicca

Wicca is a Neo-pagan religion that was introduced to the public in the 20th century by Gerald Gardner, a descendant of Grissel Gairdner, a "witch" who was persecuted and burned in 1610. Gardner was interested in the Theosophical Society, a worldwide association advocating the revival of the principle that all religions and philosophies possess an aspect of universal truth. Its motto is: "There is no religion higher than Truth." He also wrote the first book of the Wiccan ritual, *The Book of Shadows*, and in 1959, *The Meaning of Witchcraft* .

Gardner did not claim to be the founder of Wicca, but rather the initiator of a small group who perpetuated the old traditions of the Middle Ages. He founded the New Forest coven and appointed Dorothy Clutterbuck as its leading member.

Traditional Wicca

Wicca followers are called Wiccans. They believe in two divinities, the Goddess and the God, which are seen as the complementary opposites of nature. Wicca practitioners have autonomy. As it is not a dogmatic practice, each follower has their own vision and practice of Wicca.

Origins

The word Wicca comes from the verb *wiccan*, an old English word meaning "to bewitch" or "to practise magic". Gerald Gardner defined Wicca as meaning "wisdom" or "craft of the wise".

Wicca was mainly spread by American feminists in English-speaking countries, and is recognized as a religion in Canada, the United States and the United Kingdom. It is, above all, a philosophy that incorporates different movements such as environmentalism and the protection of animals.

Eclectic Wicca

While traditional Wicca is the most well-known, there are many branches of Wicca, particularly eclectic Wicca, which have a more personal and solitary approach. Traditionally, an individual has to be initiated by a coven before being able to practise. But if you follow the eclectic path, you come to Wicca through self-initiation and so do not have to be initiated by an institution.

The most well-known author on eclectic Wicca is Scott Cunningham. In his works, he argued for a free and uncomplicated Wicca that follows one of the fundamental principles of witchcraft: not to recognize any supreme authority beyond the forces of nature.

The thirteen precepts of witchcraft

Modern Wicca is based on thirteen precepts set out in 1974 by the American Council of Witches. These are principles that practitioners can draw on, use and adapt to suit their needs, wherever they are on their personal journey.

1. We practise rites to attune ourselves with the natural rhythm of life forces marked by the phases of the Moon and the seasonal Quarters and Cross Quarters.

2. We recognize that our intelligence gives us a unique responsibility towards our environment. We seek to live in harmony with nature, in biological balance offering fulfilment to life and consciousness within an evolutionary concept.

3. We acknowledge a depth of power far greater than that is apparent to the average person. Because it is far greater than ordinary it is sometimes called "supernatural", but we see it as lying within that which is naturally potential to all.

4. We conceive of the creative power in the universe as manifesting through polarity – as masculine and feminine – and that this same creative power lies in all people, and functions through the interaction of the masculine and feminine. We value neither above the other, knowing each to be supportive of the other. We value sex as pleasure, as the symbol and embodiment of life, and as one of the sources of energies used in magical practice and religious worship.

There isn't just one way

We cannot compare science with spirituality. Your practices cannot be defined as the unique and absolute truth, but as your own personal truth.

5. We recognize both outer and inner, or psychological, worlds – sometimes known as the spiritual world, the collective unconscious, inner planes, etc. – and we see in the interaction of these two dimensions the basis for paranormal phenomena and magical exercises. We therefore neglect neither dimension for the other, seeing both as necessary for our fulfilment.

6. We do not recognize any authoritarian hierarchy, but do honour those who teach, respect those who share their knowledge and wisdom, and acknowledge those who are courageously leading groups.

7. We see religion, magic and wisdom-in-living as being united in the way one views the world and in the philosophy of life which we identify as paganism.

8. Calling oneself "pagan" or "witch" does not make one so – but neither does heredity itself, nor the collecting of titles, degrees and initiations. A "witch" seeks to control the forces within her/himself that make life possible in order to live wisely and well without harm to others and in harmony with nature.

9. We believe in the affirmation and fulfilment of life in a continuation of evolution and development of consciousness, that gives meaning to the universe we know, and our personal role within it.

10. Our only animosity towards Christianity, or toward any other religion or philosophy of life, is to the extent that its institutions have claimed to be "the only way," and have sought to deny freedom to others and to suppress other ways of religious practice and belief.

11. As witches today, we are not threatened by debates on our history, our origins or our traditions. We are concerned with our present and our future.

12. We do not accept the concept of absolute evil, nor do we worship any entity known as "Satan" or "the Devil", as defined by Christian tradition. We do not seek power through the suffering of others, nor do we accept that personal benefit can be derived only by denial to another.

13. We believe that we should seek within nature that which is contributory to our health and well-being.

Three founding principles

Magic should be approached with respect, benevolence and humility, the golden values that will allow you to achieve fulfilment and positive development in your practice.

The principle of intention

In magic, we very often work with intention, and it is vital that this is "pure", because otherwise there is a risk of falling into black magic. How can we have pure intention in a world where we are constantly preoccupied by ego, jealousy, desire, worries or fears? If you uphold the values of benevolence, honesty and love, all will be well. The Thirteen Precepts of Witchcraft will help keep you on this path (see page 12).

Setting an intention is the art of communicating the desire that all will be well and letting the universe handle the outcome. For example, if you do not perform a ritual at exactly the right time of the moon, it does not matter as long as your intention is pure.

Etiquette toward invoked divinities

Although the world of divinities is a high vibrational plane, we must treat all planes with the same respect and consideration. Making a request to the divinities is vain and the result of a fragile and overinflated ego. A desire that comes from the heart is not a request.

1. In any invocation ritual, be respectful and considerate: first greet and then present yourself to the divinities.

2. Bring an offering, in the same way you might bring flowers and a bottle of wine to dinner with friends, then clearly state the reason for your invocation.

3. Do not invoke when highly emotional – this is the equivalent of entering someone's house while shouting.

4. Once the invocation is finished, be thankful that the divinities have granted you this moment, offer a parting salutation, and finish your ritual.

"Speak to humans, animals and flowers in the same way that you speak to the gods, because all is one and one is all."

The threefold law

This law stipulates that everything a person does will be returned to them three times, be it an act of benevolence or otherwise. Note that it is not for or because of this law that witches practise! Indeed, doing something with the belief that we will receive three times more "good", or not doing something out of fear of attracting three times more "bad", runs counter to the fundamental principles of magic.

In our practice, we will therefore focus on the following precept:

"Be just, and justness will follow"

Wiccan deities

The Goddess and the God

The Goddess and the God have been given so many names over the centuries that they are also known as the Nameless Ones. They represent all the deities that were born on earth and are present in many forms.

Feminine and masculine

The Goddess and the God represent feminine and masculine energies, as well as the feminine in the masculine and the masculine in the feminine, similar to yin and yang. Similarly, a part of them lives in us, and a part of us in them. That is why we can connect with them by connecting with our inner vibration.

The Goddess and the God are complementary and equal. They are the creators of all realms: plant, animal, human and ethereal.

The Goddess

The Goddess is the most commonly worshipped divinity in Wicca. Because of the patriarchal scars left by Catholicism on the world of Wicca, followers are generally more comfortable with this feminine aspect.

The Goddess represents the moon, femininity, the all-mother, wisdom and unconditional love. She is often symbolized by the triple moon, which represents the maiden, mother, and old woman as the waxing, full, and waning moon.

Symbols to honour the Goddess: cauldron, pearl, cup, mirror, necklace and silver.

The God

Commonly known as the Horned God, he is the guardian of wildlife. He is the complementary opposite of the Goddess and represents the sun. This is the radiant light that brings new life and allows it to thrive. He is slightly less revered than the Goddess because he is wrongly confused with the one God of the Catholic religion.

Symbols to honour the God: horns, sickle, magic wand, swords, candle, and gold and copper.

Other divinities

Hecate

Now an iconic Wiccan figure, Hecate is a goddess of the Greek pantheon, the daughter of Titan Perses and Titaness Asteria.

Known as the Moon Goddess, she is one part of the triple goddess, together with Selene and Artemis. Selene represents the full moon, the maturity of life. Artemis symbolizes the crescent moon, the birth of life, and Hecate is the dark moon, or new moon, representing revival and rebirth.

Hecate is honoured because she enables the passage between the three planes of the universe: the underworld, the earth and the heavens. She is also the goddess of darkness, of the world beyond the veil of life. In Wicca, she is the mother of witches, the goddess of witchcraft and primary magic. She is the emblem of mystical and occult practices. In the symbol of the triple goddess, she is the old woman, the crone, the wise woman.

Ambivalent, Hecate can be a healer or avenger, protective and loving, or ruthless and authoritarian. As a mother, she is uncompromising, but still a teacher and a healer to her children. She has experienced the world and life, and has unveiled their mysteries and wisdom. As such, she is clairvoyant and instinctively knows the truth, so there is no use trying to lie to her!

Above laws, ethics and human morality, her acts may sometimes seem disconcerting, because they serve neither good nor bad. She enforces the laws of the universe and commands the fate of souls.

Brigid

Brigid, Brigit or even Brighid is a goddess from Celtic culture. The goddess of flame, blacksmiths and smithcraft, she is associated with transformations, because her flames shape metals so that they can be used by humankind.

Connected with learning, culture and poetry, she also plays more mystical roles such as divination, wisdom and prophecies. The goddess of healing waters, medicine and childbirth, she is called the Great Teacher.

Brigid is the triple goddess of fire: the hearth, the forge, and the fire of creation. She is a shapeshifting goddess who can take any form from any kingdom: animal, mineral and vegetable. When Brigid transforms into a human, she takes a feminine appearance.

Brigid is also a sun goddess who is honoured at Imbolc, when the sun returns after the darkness of winter.

The Green Man

Seldom mentioned in written works, the Green Man, or Leaf Man, is a very ancient figure. Surprisingly, however, his representations can be found in distinct cultures.

He is the most powerful spirit of nature, the protector of gardeners, herbalists and druids. Connected with nature, fauna (especially birds), flora and spring, he is the symbol of vitality, wisdom and the slow cycle of the seasons. In winter, he disappears by returning to the earth and then reappears in spring.

He rarely appears for men and remains neutral towards them as long as the rules of etiquette are observed. He is neither vengeful nor an uncompromising teacher like the goddesses. If he is not approached with respect, he will not divulge his wisdom, and will punish with his indifference.

Teaching gentleness and patience, the Green Man is one of the most beautiful symbols of the father: gentle, benevolent and protective.

Offerings

Offerings are benevolent gifts offered to divinities, but should not be seen as a mandatory mark of our devotion to them. Like the Goddess and the God, we are all free and equal, with no other duty of devotion than the love of life.

The different offerings

Offerings are either feminine or masculine (in terms of energy, not gender).

NATURAL OFFERINGS

These are the original offerings, those that are closest to nature and respect the cycle of the seasons. Natural offerings can be seasonal fruits, vegetables, meals, berries and nuts.

Type of offering	Feminine energy	Masculine energy
Natural	Egg shell, walnut, snail shell, seashell, berry	Fruit, stone, wood, horn
Material	Cauldron, mirror, cup, chalice	Wand, sword, lance, candle
Intangible	Flower incense	Incense (frankincense, myrrh, benzoin)

MATERIAL OFFERINGS

These can be used to honour feminine and masculine energies. Their aim is not so much to offer thanks, as with offerings that come from nature, but to manifest energies. These can be precious objects or small trinkets that are important to you.

INTANGIBLE OFFERINGS

Intangible offerings are prayers, but also our attitude. Being aligned with love, benevolence and gratitude is surely the most beautiful offering we can make, because that is how we progress toward a more healthy humanity. Consider using incense in such instances, because smoke is the manifestation of the ethereal.

When to make an offering

The best time to make offerings is whenever you feel like it!

OCCASIONAL OFFERINGS

You will make offerings during your rituals, but not always. Offerings can be made during major life events, for example the birth of a child or the death of a loved one, and at other important moments when you are asking for support.

SABBATS

Sabbats are festivals during which we overflow with gratitude. We pour out our love with offerings. We celebrate the cycle of life and the seasons by honouring the magic of existence. On these occasions, offerings are an integral part of the ritual.

Witch's secret

Leave part of your meal as an offering. That way, you will be offering something that is essential for you, which you have prepared. This kind of offering has the greatest meaning.

The witch's toolkit

Magical tools

It is important to recognize that it is not the tools that make the witch, but the other way round! A gold billhook, an amethyst chalice and a wand of precious wood do not make the practitioner.

Wand — Fire/Air

The most well-known witch's tool, the wand is used to direct, concentrate and channel our force toward a specific target.

It is traditionally used during rituals, to cast magic circles, mix potions in cauldrons, or for healing.

The wand represents force, will, and skill at communicating in the different energy planes. It is depicted as a baton in the tarot card of The Magician, symbolizing communication and mediation between the physical and spiritual worlds.

The wand is associated either with the element of fire, in connection with the God, force, and the power of action; or with the element of air, as it is made from the branch of a carefully selected tree that will have been buffeted by the wind and therefore intrinsically imbued with this element.

Witch's secret

Traditionally wands are made from elder or hazel, but you may chose other woods to suit your purpose:

· *Purification and prosperity:* birch
· *Love:* apple
· *Healing:* ash
· *Protection:* rowan
· *Communication with the afterlife:* yew
· *Lunar ritual:* willow

MAKING A WAND

There are good wandmakers around, but I advise making your own, selecting a branch with care and consideration. As you take the branch, exercise profound gratitude toward nature.

• **If you are taking a cutting from a tree,** be sure to take it mindfully, and apply some of your saliva to the tree's wound. In this way, you offer the tree a tiny part of yourself in exchange for the branch.

• **If you find the branch on the ground,** purify it with sage smoke before use, and consider decorating it, so that it is imbued with your energy.

Make your own!

In ancient times, witches and wizards were men and women who were close to nature and its magic. They used basic materials to make their own tools, so don't hesitate to make your own too or call on local craftspeople.

ELDER TREE

The elder is one of the most well-known trees in magical traditions. Connected with the moon goddess, it is charged with feminine energy. The companion of Pan, god of the forest and the animal world, the Elder Mother is the guardian of the fairies and endows the tree with her magical virtues.

The elder is connected with the afterlife because it symbolizes the thirteenth moon and Samhain. It therefore links the end of a cycle and the beginning of another.

> Young elder branches are easy to hollow out when wandmaking.
> Keeping the hollowed-out centre empty focuses the wand on owner's energy.
> Filling the centre with flowers, crystals or incense increases its power.

HAZEL TREE

The Celts considered hazel trees to be sacred, and engraved oghams, the magical letters of the druids, on their branches.

A symbol of fecundity and fertility, a hazel tree planted in front of the house promised a fruitful future for young couples. In Wiccan tradition, the hazel is the tree of knowledge and wisdom.

Its straight branches are perfect for wandmaking. As with the elder, they can be hollowed out to focus the energy, although elder branches aren't as easy to hollow as elder.

Connected with the element of water by its magnetic properties, the hazel is a favourite with water diviners.

Broom — Air/Earth

According to tradition, this magical tool gives witches the power to fly, but not in the true sense of the word! The broom represents the separation of the body and the spirit, the vehicle that protects the witch on their astral journey.

Traditionally, brooms are made with the following components:
> The handle is made from the ash tree, which symbolizes air.
> The twigs from the birch tree, which symbolizes earth.
> The ties that connect the handle and the twigs are made of willow, which symbolizes the moon.

Before helping our spirit to fly, the broom is used primarily to clean the sacred space before a ritual. It is also used to activate the magic of sexuality.

Cauldron — Water/Fire

Along with the wand and broom, the cauldron is one of the most emblematic tools of witchcraft and the magical world. It symbolizes the womb, the source of life, wisdom and maternity. It also represents resurrection because it transforms ingredients during the cooking process.

Its round and hollow form, which enables it to hold solid and liquid ingredients, makes the cauldron sacred and connected with the Goddess. It is therefore associated with the element of water, the source of life. However, given that heat is needed to produce a cauldron, it is also sometimes connected with the element of fire.

It is traditionally used to create potions, put out ritual candles, or to stir consecrated ingredients for a ritual.

Grimoire

In Wiccan tradition, this was known as the book of shadows. The traditional name is a little misleading as it seems to suggest dark and ill-intentioned spells, so we will call it a grimoire. Your grimoire will contain your herbarium, your prayers, your studies and your dreams. Choose your grimoire mindfully, because you will keep it throughout your life. Choose, if possible, a grimoire made from natural material, that will have a higher magical vibration.

Athame — Air

This is traditionally a double-edged dagger that is blunted to avoid accidents during rituals. Its double-edged aspect represents life and death, construction and creation. The athame is not designed to cut materials, but is solely used to cast magic circles or sever harmful connections.

An athame's handle is traditionally black, made from wood, bone or horn, and its blade is steel, but this is not mandatory. The important thing is that you feel called by it and in accord with its vibration.

 *Altar*

The altar is central to magical practice, but you don't need an altar made from precious wood with a gold inlay to practise your magic. Altars can be created at home or in nature from whatever materials are available to you.

Creating an altar

• **At home:** your altar can be a small table, a plank of wood, or even a cloth that you like. The altar is placed at the centre of your magic circle to increase its intensity.

• **Outdoors:** outdoor altars are generally more powerful because they are in direct contact with the terrestrial forces. Creating an altar in a garden or forest is ideal, but you can also create a temporary outdoor altar in situ using a small portable wooden plank and whatever materials are available to you.

Elements representing the Goddess	Centre	Elements representing the God
Bell Chalice Gold or cream candle Cup of water	Cauldron Incense burner Seasonal flowers and fruits Pentacle Offering plate or tray	Magic wand Athame Red, yellow or gold candle Bowl of earth or salt

Decorating an altar

Traditionally, the altar is divided in two with the left dedicated to the Goddess and the right to the God. The centre of the altar symbolizes the place where the two energies meet, and it is here that you place your offerings.

When you have created and set up your altar, it is important to make an offering before practising any magic. Place fruits, flowers, a stone or artefacts on your offering tray, then take a moment to connect with this magical space. Offer thanks and then start your magical practice.

The travel altar

The travel altar is very useful when travelling or on nature walks. It is designed to be easy to carry and to allow for spontaneity.

Simply place a few essential ritual items in a small box that you can carry about with you. Choose a box that you are particularly attached to, that holds meaning for you. Feel free to decorate it to suit you.

Place all the necessary items inside your box. As with the traditional altar, take a moment to connect with its magic, then place an offering on it and leave it overnight. Your travel altar is then ready to use.

In my box

- A tea light.
- A few matches to light the tea light.
- Selenite for cleansing.
- Tourmaline for grounding and protection.
- A pentacle for protection (in steel or a disc of wood on which you draw your pentacle).
- A bag of salt to represent the earth.
- A small metal or clay cup.
- Benzoin or frankincense.
- A small rectangle of fabric.

Colours in magic

Colours are very important in magic. During rituals, the colours of the candles, cloths and decorations are chosen according to their symbolism, which varies by culture. Humankind has many associations with colours, such as the seven colours of the rainbow, which correspond to the seven days of the week, the planets, the elements, the organs, and even musical notes.

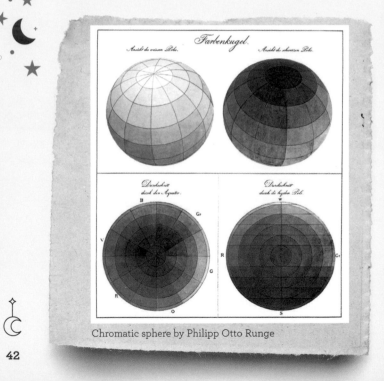

Chromatic sphere by Philipp Otto Runge

The chromatic sphere

The chromatic sphere is important for helping us to understand the symbolism of colours. This 3D sphere is made up of a black pole (South) and a white pole (North), a green axis (West) and a red axis (East), which are therefore opposites.

The symbolism of colours

PINK

A mix of red (sensuality) and white (purity), pink symbolizes the body, the soul, unity, love, the essence of being, youth and vulnerability. It represents the mother, femininity and fertility, and brings abundance and prosperity.

RED

Red is the colour of fire and blood. Associated with the planet Mars, it symbolizes force, vitality, power, sexuality, ardour, beauty, health and wealth. Red is connected with judgement and encourages action and courage. It represents the masculine principle (yang) and the heart and libido, as well as the mysteries of life, secret sciences and esoteric knowledge.

ORANGE

Orange is midway between yellow and red. It symbolizes and celebrates joy, emotion, rhythm and movement. Orange is also a point of balance between the spirit and the libido; if the balance is lost, it symbolizes lust and infidelity that arise from the imbalance. A symbol of the revelation of divine love, it encourages the expression of faith.

YELLOW

Yellow is the warmest colour, it represents gold and the sun. Associated with mystery and renewal, it symbolizes divine power, light, life, force, clarity, the awakening of the spirit, self-esteem and eternity. Yellow is attributed to royal power and prompts thoughts on the divine origin of power and the importance of kings and emperors (such as the sun). Associated with Venus and sometimes divine, sometimes earthly, yellow stimulates the imagination.

GREEN

Green represents spring, the plant kingdom, and purifying and regenerative waters. It is the colour of tolerance, initiation, awakening, life, peace and balance. It symbolizes force, hope, longevity, justice, hope, vision, the mother and refuge. In certain cultures, green is associated with water and represents the feminine principle (yin), while red represents the masculine principle (yang). In Wiccan tradition, the Goddess is generally represented by a green candle and the God by a red candle.

BLUE

Blue is the coldest colour. Often represented in transparent form (air and water), it is considered intangible. Blue represents breath, oxygen, wind and air, and symbolizes attentiveness, exchange, dreams, and the doorway between the conscious and the unconscious. It evokes ideas of tranquillity, eternity and indifference, and represents the sky separating humankind from the divine. Associated with Jupiter, blue is connected with meditation and introspection. Often equated with spirituality and the sacred, blue fosters reflection and symbolizes the renunciation of the material world and the soul's ascension to the divine.

PURPLE

Purple symbolizes lucidity, reflection, destiny, guidance, contemplation, sacrifice, the word and the father. It is a point of balance between the spirit and the senses, reflection and passion, love and wisdom, the heavens and the earth (blue and red). Its season is autumn, which marks the passage from life to death.

WHITE

White symbolizes wholeness, unity, beginnings and endings. It is intrinsically linked with the transformation of the being, with initiation, death and rebirth. The colour of purity, it symbolizes innocence, revelation and mercy. Associated with the moon, it gives rise to the spirit.

GREY

Associated with Mercury, grey represents the unconscious, transition, resurrection, sadness and melancholy. It is at the centre of the chromatic sphere and is a combination of black and white, which symbolize humankind and thought.

BLACK

In its cold and negative form, black symbolizes darkness, passiveness, death, chaos, obscurity and impurity. Like white, it is associated with the North-South axis and the ends of the poles. Symbolizing

Fire	Red, orange
Water	Green
Air	Yellow, white
Earth	Black

the centre of the earth, black evokes its fertility and embodies rebirth and hope. In an initiatory death, it represents the challenge that brings us to the path of light. Associated with Saturn, black promotes intelligence.

45

The magic circle

The magic circle comprises a geometric form (pentagram), called sacred geometry, surrounded by a circle (pentacle) symbolizing the cosmic man.

What is a magic circle?

A pentagram is a five-point star formed of continuous lines of equal length. Pentacle is the term given to a circle surrounding a symbol such as a square, star or triangle. These two geometric forms are used in different ways: the pentacle's circle, which surrounds the pentagram, symbolizes unity and evokes protection. A magic circle marks the separation between the material and spiritual worlds (the profane and the sacred). The pentacle acts as a platform for receiving energies.

The purpose of the magic circle

Depending on the energies being called upon, a pentagram, pentacle or a magic circle can be used for protection, banishment or healing, and also to ward off influences or open your perception. The symbol itself is not protective; only the circle and the energies invoked bring their forces.

Casting the magic circle

To invite the cardinal directions or the elements to join you, cast a circle on the ground around your altar in a clockwise direction. The circle must be big enough for you to be able to move inside it. You can cast the circle with your finger, your wand or your athame while visualizing it in your mind, or with chalk if you want to draw it physically.

Casting a pentagram and pentacle

A pentagram can be visualized or "drawn" using your wand or athame, engraved on a natural material, or drawn physically on paper or parchment.

MATERIALS: paper, pencil, compass, ruler, rubber (eraser).

1. Lightly draw a circle that can easily be rubbed out, then, using a ruler, draw the vertical and horizontal diameter. Place the points E and F in the middle of segments OB and OD.

2. Taking point A as the centre of a circle with the radius AE, mark the intersecting points G and H.

3. Take points G and H as the centres of circles with the radius GA and HA, and mark points I and J.

4. Rub out the lines, including the circle, and connect points AI, AJ, GH, GJ and HI to create a five-point star.

5. If you wish to add a pentacle, simply draw a circle around the pentagram.

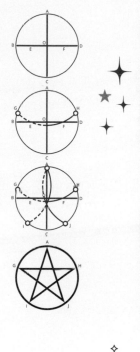

The four elements

Fire

Planets	Sun, Mars
Signs	Leo, Sagittarius, Aries
Deities	Brigid, Freyja, Ra, Horus, Prometheus, Morrigan, Indra
Plants	Cinnamon, basil, nettle
Crystals	Carnelian, garnet, red jasper, agate, quartz
Colour	Red
Powers	Love, sexuality, protection, purification, transformation, force, courage

The element of fire symbolizes sexuality and passion, and promotes intuition. Uncontrollable and destructive, it is the most dangerous element, and so should be handled with care. Fire is associated with the sun, light and lightning. It expresses superior force, passion, knowledge, intuition and desire. In magic, it symbolizes acts and events. This element is called on when carrying out rituals associated with sudden changes and the immediate need for energy.

Water	
Planet	Moon
Signs	Pisces, Cancer, Scorpion
Deities	Osiris, Isis, Neptune, Aphrodite
Plants	Chamomile, lotus, lilac, fern, rose, deadly nightshade, lettuce
Crystals	Moonstone, lapis lazuli, aquamarine, blue topaz
Colour	Blue
Powers	Psychic powers, purification, the sacred feminine, dreams, healing, reflection

The element of water symbolizes the spiritual life, the source of all life. Water is associated with the moon. It is connected with the unconscious, dreams and the imagination. It evokes the cycles of life, and corresponds with the soul and religion. In magic, it symbolizes the emotions, dreams and intimacy. This element is called on when carrying out rituals associated with feelings of love and reconciliation.

49

Air	
Planets	Jupiter, Venus
Signs	Gemini, Libra, Aquarius
Deities	Nyx, Hermes, Athena
Plants	Benzoin, frankincense, lavender, yarrow, aniseed, verbena
Crystals	Topaz, aventurine, amethyst
Colour	Yellow
Powers	Purification, intuition, psychic power, memory, creativity

The element of air symbolizes spirituality. It is associated with wind and breath. It represents the invisible life and the subtle world. It is a means of communication between the earth and the heavens. It corresponds to the mind and philosophy. Purifying, the element of air symbolizes communication, exchange and relationships. Air is called on when carrying out rituals associated with creativity and community.

Earth

Planets	Saturn, Mercury
Signs	Taurus, Virgo, Capricorn
Deities	Gaia, Dionysus, Demeter, Athos, Pan
Plants	Cedar, willow, cypress
Crystals	Onyx, tiger eye, tourmaline, quartz, jasper
Colour	Green
Powers	Abundance, prosperity, physical force, fertility, growth, material gain

The element of earth symbolizes the mother, the origin of all things. Often represented by goddesses, it is associated with nurturing and fecundity. The element of earth corresponds with the body and material life. Symbolizing physical and material presence, as well as the senses, it is called on when performing rituals concerning prosperity, material gain, the land and the harvests.

Aether

The four elements come from aether; the fluid that surrounds the cosmos. Also known as quintessence, aether symbolizes the spirit, the divine, and is considered to be energy in pure form.

Invoking the cardinal directions

• **North:** located to the right of the sun, the North is associated with earth. It symbolizes fertility, wisdom, knowledge, teaching, patience and truth.

• **South:** located to the left of the sun, the South is associated with fire. It symbolizes energy, transformation, force, passion and desire.

• **East:** the East is associated with air. It symbolizes movement, inspiration, illumination, the conscious, philosophy, perception, ideas, communication and the spirit.

• **West:** the West is associated with water and symbolizes fluidity, healing, emotions, health and peace.

1. Once you have cast your circle, place four white candles, which you will light during your invocation. You could also use the following to represent the cardinal directions:
   - **East:** air can be represented by incense.
   - **South:** fire is represented by a candle.
   - **West:** water is represented by a chalice filled with water.
   - **North:** earth can be represented by a bowl of soil, a plant or salt.

2. To invoke the cardinal directions, say:

   "East, South, West, North, I invoke your presence!"

3. Light the East candle and say:

   "Guardian of the East, give me the breath of your force."

4. Light the South candle and say:

   "Guardian of the South, give me the fire of your power."

5. Light the West candle and say:

   "Guardian of the West, let your cosmic water give me energy."

6. Finish by lighting the North candle and say:

   "Guardian of the North, fertilize my spirit and bring me truth."

Witch's secret

The incantations here are suggestions. When you feel you need to invoke, do so with your own words and an open heart.

Invoking the elements

The direction in which the arms of the pentagram are cast is important, as is the direction in which the pentacle circle is cast. Casting the latter in a clockwise direction evokes invitation; anticlockwise evokes banishment.

1 Aether

4 Air

3 Water

2 Earth

5 Fire

1. **Calling upon the element of aether:** start with aether (1), move on to earth (2), then water (3), air (4), fire (5) and lastly, return to aether (1).

2. **Calling upon the element of water:** start with water (3), move on to air (4), followed by fire (5), aether (1), earth (2) and lastly, return to water (3).

3. **Calling upon the element of fire:** start with fire (5), move on to aether (1), followed by earth (2), water (3), air (4) and lastly, return to fire (5).

4. **Calling upon the element of earth:** start with earth (2), move on to water (3), followed by air (4), fire (5), aether (1) and lastly, return to earth (2).

5. **Calling upon the element of air:** start with air (4), move on to fire (5), followed by aether (1), earth (2), water (3) and lastly, return to air (4).

Dispelling the magic circle

1. When you have completed your ritual, take a few moments to thank the elements and the cardinal directions for their presence, starting with the East and finishing with the North:

> *"I thank you, Guardian of the East, ruler of air, for your presence, for the force you have given me, and for the protection you have provided."*

2. Repeat for each direction.

3. To finish, dispel your circle in an anticlockwise direction, saying:

> *"May the energies disperse, may they return to earth, air, water, fire and aether. May it be so."*

Activating the pentacle

To activate your pentacle or pentagram, take a few minutes to meditate before you begin to help focus your intention. Put all of your energy into its creation. When joining up the points (elements), visualize each of them in turn and the overall creation of the symbol.

Best practices in magic

Alignment and justness

The most important thing in magical practice is to focus on personal alignment and justness. While it's difficult to be constantly "just", it's important to work on this as often as possible. Here are a few practices to include in your daily routine to help you be as aligned as possible with justness.

Staying just

Striving for justness is important if we are to avoid falling into the ego trap and becoming drawn to vengeful magic. Remember that every act has its consequences. Live by the values of benevolence, love and friendship, and you will receive the just reward. However, should your values be hatred, vengeance and sabotage, you will also receive the just consequences.

What is justness?

It is important to understand the difference between good, bad and just. In magic (as in any energy practice), the notion of good and bad is fairly abstract. It would be presumptuous to assert that we know exactly what is good and what is not. For example, doing an incantation thinking that it is "good" may have good consequences, but could equally have very bad consequences. It is therefore important to connect with what we consider just, which is neither good nor bad.

"Not helping someone, is sometimes helping them." Start by doing things for you, and over the years, as you gain experience and wisdom, you will be able to perhaps think about supporting others. Remember that like nature, the Goddess and the God, we must be humble before the greatness of the magic of life.

 **Breathing**

Before every practice, take a moment to relax, breathe and release any tension.

Try these exercises first thing in the morning to start the day feeling connected, before a ritual or before going on a nature walk. Or practice before going to bed to release stress and promote restful sleep.

Deep breathing

1. Get into a comfortable position, either sitting, standing or lying down.

2. Place your left hand on your stomach, just below your navel. Your left hand represents the Goddess, your feminine and creative energy, and the abundance of the earth in you.

3. Place your right hand on your chest, half way between the hollow of your clavicle and the bottom of your sternum. Your right hand represents the God, your creative and masculine energy, and the power of the sun in you.

4. Inhale deeply and slowly, inflating your stomach. Feel that you are nourishing your inner Goddess, your earth. Exhale through your mouth, deflating your stomach.

5. Inhale slowly and deeply once more, this time inflating your chest. Feel that you are nourishing your interior God, your sun.

In the morning, repeat three times: Goddess inhale/exhale/ God inhale/exhale. At night, continue until you fall asleep.

Alternate nostril breathing

1. Sit comfortably with your legs crossed.

2. Place your left hand on your left knee.

3. Close your eyes and inhale deeply through both nostrils.

4. Close your right nostril with the thumb of your right hand.

5. Exhale through your left nostril for a count of eight, to cleanse your earth and your femininity, and to purify the Goddess in you.

6. Inhale through your left nostril for a count of four, keeping your right nostril closed. As you inhale, feel your Goddess being nourished and growing.

7. Now alternate by closing your left nostril with the ring finger of your right hand.

8. Exhale through your right nostril for a count of eight, to cleanse your light, your masculinity, and to purify the God within you.

9. Inhale through your right nostril for a count of four, keeping the left nostril closed. As you inhale, feel your God being nourished and your sun growing.

Grounding

Grounding is our connection with the earth. In energy and magical practices, we tend to focus on our spiritual connection and can overlook our earthly connection. Grounding techniques can help us to maintain a bond with the natural world around us and stay tuned to our own emotions.

Grounding to connect with the earth

This quick grounding technique can be performed anywhere, before any practice. It is best to do this exercise barefoot while standing outside, if possible. If inside, stand on a small rug.

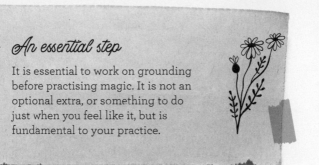

An essential step

It is essential to work on grounding before practising magic. It is not an optional extra, or something to do just when you feel like it, but is fundamental to your practice.

1. Stand with your feet hip-width apart.

2. Inhale deeply and bring your awareness to your feet. Feel their force, supporting the weight of your body, and their heaviness.

3. Become aware of your arches and their contact with the ground. Imagine the sweet dampness of the earth beneath you. Feel the benevolence of the earth, which allows everything to be born and to grow.

4. Now imagine your feet sprouting roots that anchor you to the ground.

5. With every inhale, feel the energy rising up your roots, and with every exhale, feel your energy connect with the ground beneath you.

6. Once this connection is established, you will no longer feel any heaviness in your feet, but simply a sensation of intense stability.

Projection

Astral projection, or an out-of-body experience, is a practice that enables you to visit planes other than your own, to go and search for information, and, for the more advanced, to go and visit other times and eras.

An advanced practice

Projection is not recommended for beginners – you really need to be skilled in grounding techniques and in your alignment beforehand. Do not try projection before this, otherwise you risk losing your connection with reality.

Projection is not a dream or a lucid dream (the capacity to control our dreams and consciously interact with them). It is also not simply a journey of the spirit, but also of the astral body, the energy body similar to our physical body but on a non-physical plane.

- **Intentional projection:** projection that we have sought and we control. It will be desired but will be no less dangerous because, without careful protection and grounding, it unfortunately leaves us open to possession.

- **Unintentional projection:** either you experience this projection because your energy is in a healthy and pure vibration, and life invites you to move onto the next level in your journey, or because you are so ungrounded that you can no longer remain in your body.

Meditation

Meditation channels our focus on our spirit, body or emotions. It invites us to journey ever further along our path to personal development, the basis of any magical practice. It is often wrongly thought that meditation is the art of thinking of nothing, of emptying the mind. However, meditation is more the art of cleansing and organizing our spirit, of thinking "better", of emptying it of obstructions and restrictive thoughts. Grounding and breathing exercises are forms of meditation.

Purification

Purification is the act of cleansing yourself, your home or your magical objects of residual energy. Over time, we become charged with the energy traces of our experiences, our encounters and our emotions.

Mindful shower

Water has the power to cleanse and clear matter and energy. Elevate your morning shower to a sacred moment with this purifying ritual.

1. Whilst in the shower, take time to cleanse your mind, body, emotions and energy.

2. Consider water a beneficial source, washing away residual energy and emotions.

3. You can do the same thing for your magical objects by running them under the tap while visualizing the cleansing of non-beneficial energy.

Try this ritual using natural water sources such as rivers, waterfalls, the sea or the ocean.

Smoke bath

Cleanse yourself and
your magical objects
with this purifying
smoke ritual using
common sage or bay
leaves – locally grown
if possible – incense,
resins or wood.

1. Gently light the item to be
burned using the flame of your altar candle.

2. Allow it to flame for a moment then place it in a cup.
Put out the flame by shaking it gently.

3. Consciously wave the cup all around you. Better yet,
place it on the ground and step over it.

4. Pass your objects through the smoke.

Note

Avoid using palo santo or white sage for
this ritual. Although effective, there are
sustainability issues with both and there
are plenty of alternatives to choose from.

Salt purification

Salt is one of the oldest purification tools. It dispels negative energy from all places, objects and people.

• **For yourself:** dissolve unrefined coarse salt in your bath water.

• **For your objects:** leave your object overnight in a cup of unrefined coarse salt.

• **For your home:** place two cups filled with coarse salt on either side of your door, or in each corner of your home. Alternatively bury small linen bags filled with coarse salt at the four corners of the land on which you live.

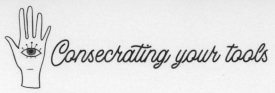 *Consecrating your tools*

Use this ritual to consecrate your tools and altar before their first use. Consecrate each object one by one, rather than all at the same time.

Consecration by the elements

Consecrating a tool involves presenting it to the energies and/or the Goddess and God, and clearly expressing its purpose. It will then be cleansed of any remaining energy residues. It is an intense moment of connection between the practitioner and the divine energies, in which the tool transforms from mere objects to magical entities.

1. Cast your magic circle with your athame.

2. Place the following items into the circle, in this order:
   - A cup of salt to the North, to symbolize earth.
   - A cup of incense to the East, to symbolize air.
   - A candle to the South, to symbolize fire.
   - A cup of water to the West, to symbolize water.

3. Place the object to be consecrated in the middle of the circle.

4. Start with the energy of earth by taking a pinch of salt from the cup and consciously sprinkling it on your object. Say:

> *"I call on the North,*
> *and by the energy of earth,*
> *I consecrate this tool."*

5. Hold the object to be consecrated over the smoke of your incense, saying:

> *"I call on the East, and by the energy of air,*
> *I consecrate this tool."*

6. Hold your object over the flame of your candle, saying:

> *"I call on the South, and by the energy of fire,*
> *I consecrate this tool."*

7. To complete the consecration, join your fingertips together, dip them in your cup of water and sprinkle droplets on your object, saying:

> *"I call on the West, and by the energy of water,*
> *I consecrate this tool."*

8. Finally, say:

> *"Purified and consecrated,*
> *this object is dedicated to harmony*
> *and for the good of all.*
> *So may it be."*

Recharging objects
(STONES AND DIVINATION TOOLS)

Stones and divination tools need to be frequently bathed in terrestrial energies to recharge their energy and ensure their effectiveness.

Full moon bath

The most traditional way to recharge your stones and tools is to give them a full moon bath.

1. Place your stones and tools in a hessian (burlap) bag.

2. Three days before a full moon, place the bag in a slow-flowing river. Weight it down, and leave it for seven days.

The objects will be purified and recharged by the energies of water, earth, air and fire, by the sun and by the moon.

The
RITUALS

The eight annual sabbats

🌙 *Yule* ★ DECEMBER

Yule is the winter solstice, the darkest time and the longest night of the year. This sabbat is on 21 December.

A bit of history

The word *yule* is Norwegian in origin and means "wheel". Symbolically, it represents inner force and resilience. It marks the first day of winter and evokes the start of a new cycle as the days grow longer, heralding the birth of the sun. In the past, bonfires of joy were lit to celebrate the sun's birth. Today, these fires are mainly in our hearths, symbolizing the rebirth of the gods in the sacred fire of the Goddess. In many cultures, Yule is a period of festivities.

Why do we celebrate Yule?

This sabbat celebrates the birth of the sun. Traditionally, a Yule tree is decorated with garlands of flowers, spices, fruits and wheat to symbolize the sun, with a straw star at the top to represent the polar star. Mistletoe, a sacred plant for druids, and the pine tree are the most important plants in this celebration.

We make offerings to the spirits of nature, we help others, make donations, give gifts, feed the birds, and make delicious meals to share with family and friends. Anything made from apples, such as cider, as well as hazelnuts, walnuts, pears and spices, is perfect for the occasion.

Associations

Planets	Jupiter, sun
Elements	Fire, earth
Deities	Odin, Dionysus, Attis, Lucina, Hecate, Saturn, Freyja
Plants	Cedar, pine, rosemary, oak, holly, winter rose, ivy
Crystals	Ruby, tiger eye
Colours	Silver, gold, red, green, white

Decorating the altar

At Yule, the altar is decorated with winter plants such as holly, bay and mistletoe, as well as red and green candles. Offerings generally include walnut, apples and hazelnuts.

Cloth	White
Candles	Green, red
Tools	Cauldron, book
Symbols	Five-point star
Plants	Rosemary, bay, holly, mistletoe, cedar

The Yule ritual

On this day, we perform rituals to dispel negativity, express wishes, or ask for protection for the months ahead. It is the perfect time to take stock, draw on your inner force to promote good energies, cultivate wisdom, work on self-awareness, and undertake personal development.

MATERIALS: paper or notebook, pen, matches or lighter.

1. Once your altar is decorated and your candles lit, position yourself comfortably and meditate on the energies within you. Visualize the sun and think about the earth and the birth of life.

2. In your notebook, note down anything you would like to offload. This can be a vision, a belief, a past event, or anything of your choosing. When you have finished burn the note, visualizing the words as they disappear.

79

Imbolc ★ FEBRUARY

Celebrated on 2 February, Imbolc is a Celtic festival that honours the goddess Brigid.

A bit of history

Imbolc symbolizes the recovery of the Goddess and the birth of the young gods. It represents the purification by fire of the sun, which awakens slowly, fertilizing the earth and causing seeds to germinate.

In Wiccan tradition, this sabbat is a period in which initiation and dedication rituals are performed. It symbolizes the return of the light and access to knowledge and wisdom. During this sabbat, we consecrate the candles we will use during the year ahead, and purify our body, spirit and home. Rituals mainly focus on fertility, Mother Earth and the Sun God. At Imbolc, we also make our ritual broom.

Imbolc across civilizations

The Romans, Celts and Egyptians celebrated Imbolc on different dates, but always to honour the sun, purify places and warm the earth with bonfires. In Christianity this day is now known as Candlemas.

Why do we celebrate Imbolc?

This sabbat promotes rebirth and the fertility of the earth and of our spirits. It is the ideal time to set resolutions, develop ideas or start new projects.

Associations

Planets	Saturn, Uranus
Element	Fire
Deities	Aradia, Brigid, Junon, Frigg, Demeter
Plants	Birch, myrrh, snowdrop, bay, frankincense, sandalwood
Crystals	Garnet, amethyst, turquoise, onyx, jasper, ruby
Colours	Green, white, yellow, pink, blue, orange

Decorating the altar

Decorate your altar with white flowers and 13 candles placed in a circle to represent the 13 moons. You can place a broomstick next to the altar to symbolize purification and the act of putting aside the past.

Cloth	White, flowery
Candles	White
Tools	Ritual broom, cup, cauldron
Symbols	Milk, seeds
Plants	Pine, cedar, white blossom

Making a Brigid cross

Brigid, known as Saint Bridget in Christianity, is the most powerful and well-known goddess in Celtic mythology. The goddess of fire is associated with poetry, fertility, the forge, wisdom, healing and change, and also protects childbirth.

MATERIALS: Fourteen 50-cm (1ft 8) reed, rush or straw stems, string, container filled with water

A few days before the sabbat, make a Brigid cross as a symbol of protection, which you will use during your ritual. A Brigid cross has 4 arms of 7 stems, each representing a lunar cycle.

1. Place the stems in a container of water. Leave to soak for half an hour, then drain.

2. Place two stems in a cross shape to form a sundial (with arms at 12 o'clock, 3 o'clock, 6 o'clock and 9 o'clock).

3. Take a third stem and fold it in half over one of the horizontal arm, Fold it in the middle of the cross, toward 6 o'clock.

4. Repeat with another stem, toward 9 o'clock, then 12 o'clock and so on until you have used all the stems.

5. Tie the ends of each arm with a small piece of string.

The Imbolc ritual

Traditionally, we place a Brigid doll, crystals and candles on the altar, and express our wishes with particular focus on our intention.

MATERIAL: paper, pencil, moon water or snow water, matches or a lighter.

1. Place your Brigid cross on the altar, along with the 13 candles arranged in a circle to represent the sun.

2. Light the candles.

3. Take a few moments to meditate, then write down how you felt during your meditation on a piece of paper.

4. Allow your spirit to express itself, then state your intentions and wishes for the month ahead.

Ostara ★ MARCH

Ostara is the spring equinox, when the sun is at its zenith, directly over the equator. It is the time of year when night and day are in perfect balance.

A bit of history

In Wiccan tradition, Ostara symbolizes fertility and rebirth. It marks the awakening of nature and of the sacred feminine. In other traditions, the Green Goddess or the Lord of the Wood are honoured. This celebration was common among the Mayas, the Romans, the Saxons, and in countries such as Iran.

Why do we celebrate Ostara?

The energies of nature bring new connections with the world, so Ostara is the perfect time to reconnect with nature, new energies and our guides.

Ostara promotes the fulfilment of projects, and physical, spiritual and emotional growth. It marks the rebirth of our being, a time for cleansing and purifying. Gardening, walking, having fun, playing or listening to music are perfect activities for this day. Ostara is a good time for divination, purifying and consecrating your divination tools, and calling on the mercy of nature for good harvests.

It is a day for cooking for family and friends. Egg-based dishes such as quiches and brioches, along with recipes containing honey such as cakes or mead are given pride of place!

Associations

Planets	Jupiter, Neptune
Element	Air
Deities	Ostara, Eostre
Plants	Sage, jasmine, willow, hyacinth, mallow, verbena
Crystals	Red jasper, aquamarine, topaz
Colours	Green, yellow, pink, brown, purple

Decorating the altar

During this sabbat, we decorate our altars and homes with spring flowers. Yellow candles placed on the altar symbolize the sun. You can also place any seeds you would like to sow in the garden on the altar to bless them during the sabbat. As an offering, place eggs decorated or painted with symbols (moon, flowers, etc.) on the altar.

Cloth	Brown
Candles	Yellow
Tools	Divination tools
Symbols	Eggs, phoenix, hare, basket, seeds
Plants	Spring flowers

The Ostara ritual

The Ostara sabbat is a time for consecrating divination tools, talismans and amulets.

MATERIALS: matches or a lighter, smudge stick or incense (purification), talisman, amulets, wands, etc., divination tools (tarot, oracle, pendulum)

1. Decorate your altar, light the candles and position yourself comfortably to start your consecration ritual.

2. Place your divination tools, amulets and talismans in front of you and light your smudge stick or incense to purify them.

3. Pick up each object and consecrate it, saying a few words, such as:

"I consecrate this pendulum, with fire, water, earth and air, in the name of [name of the god or goddess, the sun, Mother Earth, etc.]."

Choose your own words for the consecration. Simply listen to your heart.

Beltane ★ MAY

The festival of fire and light, Beltane symbolizes the arrival of May and the sacred union of the God and Goddess. This celebration is held on the night of 30 April.

A bit of history

Beltane, or Beltaine, is considered the most important day in the Celtic calendar. It represents fertility, sexuality, love and vitality. This sabbat marks the arrival of the first fruits of the season and the promise of an abundant harvest. During this celebration, we decorate May Trees with ribbons, flowers and treats as a sign of friendship.

Many rituals connected with fire and water are held on this date. We light bonfires to ward off hail, late frosts and other natural disasters that may pose a risk to crops. We collect rainwater and dew to perform rituals of healing and youth.

Walpurgis Night

The night before the sabbat of Beltane is a witches' festival known as Walpurgis Night and is dedicated to the spirits of the forest. It is the perfect time to make contact with these spirits, either by going on a nature walk or performing a ritual.

Why do we celebrate Beltane?

The sabbat of Beltane celebrates fertility, prosperity, growth, creation, union, love and passion. It is a day for introspection and for getting in touch with and connecting with nature. This celebration invites us to purify ourselves and to eliminate the negative aspects of our life. It is the ideal day for divination.

Associations

Planets	Moon, Venus
Elements	Fire, water
Deities	Flora, Belenus, Pan, Cernunnos, Aphrodite, Freyja
Plants	Hawthorn, lilac, lily of the valley, willow, frankincense, daisy
Crystals	Rose quartz, celestine, amethyst, lapis-lazuli
Colours	Yellow, pink, green, purple, brown

Decorating the altar

Decorate the altar with seasonal flowers, tools and symbols representing water and fire. Offer flowers, fruits, coloured ribbons and heart-shaped biscuits. Bel Fires can be lit to purify and bless ourselves.

Cloth	Green
Candles	Red, green, pink, yellow
Tools	Cauldron, chalice, athame
Symbols	Ribbon, flower wreath
Plants	Wild flowers

The Beltane ritual

The energies of Beltane call for us to perform our ritual outside. If possible take your materials into a forest to perform this ritual.

MATERIALS: paper or notebook, pen, offerings (flowers, fruits)

1. Cast your circle, then call on the elements. Invite the spirits of the forest and the gods and goddesses to join you. Lastly, make your offerings.

2. You can also take a few moments to meditate on love and sensuality. Visualize your inner light and feel the energies around you.

The May Tree or Maypole

Since Antiquity, planting the May Tree is a fecundity rite associated with the rebirth of nature and the awakening of the earth. Holding the ends of coloured ribbons attached to the May Tree, men and women dance around it to decorate it and celebrate love and fecundity. The May Tree dance originated in Germanic paganism as a phallic symbol of fecundity and the abundance of nature.

Litha ★ JUNE

Litha is the longest day of the year, the summer solstice, which marks the apotheosis of the solar cycle. This sabbat is celebrated around 21 June.

A bit of history

Litha is a festival of rejoicing dedicated to the sun, fire, fertility and love. It symbolizes abundance, growth, prosperity, vitality and liberation. Traditionally, we light bonfires of joy (Litha Fires), which, under Christianity, have become the Bonfires of Saint John. We dance around the fires and when the embers have turned to ash, we spread them on the fields in order to bring fertility.

Why do we celebrate Litha?

At Litha, we celebrate abundance, fecundity, force, vitality, love and joy. On this date we also celebrate the renewal of nature as a whole, as well as plants, insects, etc. The veil between worlds is thin, and it is said that the spirits of nature enter our world to take advantage of the longest day of the year. It is the perfect time to communicate with them.

This day is ideal for getting outside, admiring nature, watching the sun rise and set, singing, dancing and sharing these special moments with friends and family. It is the time to take action and to calm our thoughts so that we can focus fully on our projects. It is also the perfect time for meditation to increase our awareness and intuition.

Collecting magic herbs

During Litha, we collect magical and medicinal herbs that will be used throughout the year to make potions, incense, philtres and oils. This harvesting is a sacred act, and it is believed that the effect of the plants is more powerful when they are collected on the solstice. Some must be collected at sunrise, some at midday, some at sunset, and others at night under the energies of the moon. On this day, many witches and wizards cut the branch they will use to make their wand.

Associations	
Planet	Mercury, Venus
Elements	Water, fire
Deities	Aphrodite, Freyja, Venus, Astarte
Plants	Rose, foxglove, jasmine, oak
Crystals	Aventurine, moss agate, jade
Colours	Orange, red, green, gold

Decorating the altar

For Litha, decorate the altar with ferns, sunflowers, fruits, crystals, and herbs that can be burnt to bring a delicate fragrance to your home. You can place your magical tools on it, along with symbols representing fecundity, fertility and love. Litha is the ideal day to recharge your crystals in the sun's rays.

Cloth	Red, orange
Candles	Gold
Tools	Wand, athame
Symbols	Moon, butterfly, sun, wheel, pregnant woman
Plants	Sunflower, chamomile, fern

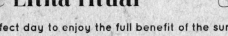

The Litha ritual

Litha is the perfect day to enjoy the full benefit of the sun: get up at dawn to see the sunrise.

MATERIALS: magical objects, wood, matches or lighter, plants and/or crystals

1. Set up your altar and gather together everything you no longer need, such as last year's plants that are too old to be used, along with the plants you wish to consecrate.

2. Light a fire in your cauldron or outside. Throw in your old plants as well as the bags, potions and dolls you made over the last year which are no longer useful.

3. Hold the objects and plants you wish to charge with the sun's energy over the flames.

4. When the fire has burnt out, collect the ash and spread it over your garden, in the soil around your plants.

Lughnasadh ★ AUGUST

This sabbat, held on 1 August, is dedicated to Lugh, the Celtic god of the sun, who taught humankind to work the fields, plant crops and harvest.

A bit of history

The festival of Lughnasadh marks the first harvest of grains that will be used to make bread flour. During this festival the Gauls used to make dolls out of wheat straw, called "wheat dolls", which were kept all year as a talisman.

Lughnasadh is one of the three sabbats dedicated to harvests. It symbolizes relief, the abundance of harvests, the approach of autumn, and the fertility of the earth. In recognition, we give some of our harvest in offering. Lughnasadh also represents friendship, peace, abundance and prosperity. For the Celts, it is a festival for celebrating community and expressing our wishes for prosperity to the sun.

Why do we celebrate Lughnasadh?

This sabbat celebrates abundance, gratitude, introspection, prosperity, our ancestors and sacrifice. It is the ideal moment to reconnect with yourself, to appreciate yourself, and to send thoughts of gratitude to nature and to friends and family.

It is also a day to clear out, cleanse and purify our environment, as well as our hearts and minds. This enables us to cast off thoughts and feelings that have become a burden. It is important to open your heart, to spend time with friends and family, and to wipe the slate clean. It is also a good time to connect with the heavens and to take up astrology and astronomy.

Associations	
Planet	Sun
Elements	Fire, water
Deities	Demeter, Ceres, Lugh, Odin
Plants	Cedar, walnut tree, mint, sage, hazel tree, rose, deadly nightshade, lavender, thyme, basil
Crystals	Malachite, red jasper, jade
Colours	Orange, yellow, green

Decorating the altar

Decorate your altar with wheat and seasonal flowers, fruits and vegetables. Place a corn doll, bread, and yellow and orange candles on the altar. It is customary to hang a wreath of wheat decorated with green ribbon on the door for prosperity and fertility.

Cloth	Embroidered with flowers
Candles	Yellow, orange
Tools	Chalice, candles, cauldron
Symbols	Pentacle, wheel, horn of abundance, corn doll
Plants	Wheat, carnations, seasonal flowers

The Lughnasadh ritual

At Lughnasadh, we make bags and potions, and perform protection spells, which are thought to be more effective when made or performed on this sacred day.

MATERIALS: 3 cotton or linen bags, paper, pen, matches or a lighter, incense or a smudge stick

1. Gather plants, crystals, seeds and any items that you consider a symbol of abundance, prosperity and self-love.

2. The bags must be made from a natural material, but the colour is your choice. The first bag will be for abundance and prosperity, the second for protection, and the third for self-love.

3. With the smoke from the incense or smudge stick, purify the bags and the items you are going to fill them with.

4. Place the flowers, crystals and seeds inside the bags, then tie them shut with ribbon or a piece of string.

Mabon ★ SEPTEMBER

Mabon celebrates the autumn equinox on 21 September. It marks the moment when days and nights are equal lengths and therefore symbolizes balance.

A bit of history

Mabon represents the harvest festival, but also the beginning of the darker period of the year. It is during this period that nature and humankind start to prepare for winter with its colder months and darker days. Perceived as a portal, it is at Mabon that the veil between worlds starts to thin until Samhain. Mabon symbolizes water, fog, old age, and endings.

Why do we celebrate Mabon?

Mabon is an ideal time to take stock, start a book of gratitude, work on karma, and think of our ancestors. It is also the perfect day to intensely purify our homes, bodies and spirits, and dispel any negative energy. We become aware that life is precious and we show gratitude for the gifts of nature.

The energies of Mabon are perfect for seeking balance, healing and grounding. Meditation, introspection, reading, and personal and spiritual development are all recommended activities. We take the time to rest and to do inner work to prepare for the darker period of the year. Organize seeds, homes and ourselves while performing a protection ritual.

Traditionally, we make corn husk dolls and talismans with leaves and pine cones, and place them on our altars.

Associations

Planet	Mercury
Element	Water
Deities	Thor, Persephone, Mabon, the Horned God
Plants	Sandalwood, carnation, hazel tree, apple tree, cypress, benzoin
Crystals	Citrine, agate, carnelian, amber, tiger eye, sapphire
Colours	Orange, yellow, brown

Decorating the altar

Dark colours represent the approaching darkness. Leaves fallen from the trees and autumn vegetables are appropriate. To symbolize prosperity and abundance, make a wreath of oak leaves and acorns.

Cloth	Black, brown
Candles	Green, brown, orange
Tools	Cauldron, chalice
Symbols	Balance (hourglass, scale), harvest (grains, roots)
Plants	Pine cone, oak leaves, walnuts, grapes, acorns

The Mabon ritual

The Mabon sabbat is the perfect time to perform a protection ritual followed by a moment of introspection.

MATERIALS: matches or a lighter, smudge stick or incense (protection), tarot or oracle, paper, pen

1. Set up your altar. Cast a circle, light the candles and meditate for a few moments.

2. Start your ritual by burning a protection incense. Cast a pentagram and call on each of the elements to bring you balance.

3. You can write down what you are feeling, what you perceive, and for what you feel grateful.

4. Lastly, take a few moments to do a card reading. The first card will represent a review of the past few months, the second will show you the things that you must finish in order to make progress. The third will prompt you to set new intentions and projects for the months ahead.

Samhain ★ OCTOBER

Samhain, also known as the Apple Festival or Halloween, is a special celebration because it is also the pagan New Year. It is the first day of the Wheel of the Year, which is celebrated on 31 October.

A bit of history

In Gaelic, Samhain means "end of summer" and evokes the transition and openness to the new world. It celebrates the final harvests and symbolizes the end of a cycle and the start of a new one; death and rebirth. Embodying the sleep of the gods, this period heralds the earth's preparation for winter and hibernation.

Celtic in origin, Samhain represents festivities and death, which is honoured with joy. Celebrations used to last seven days with the first dedicated to the memory of heroes, the second to the memory of the dead, and the rest to the festivities. The druids used to hold great feasts to celebrate the journey to rebirth and life.

Why do we celebrate Samhain?

During this sabbat, we pay homage to our ancestors, and invite them to join in the family feast. Traditionally, a plate of food is left outside the house for the dead, along with a candlestick at the window to light their path as they travel to the Summerland. Apples are buried in the ground as food for their journey.

Halloween

At Samhain, the veil between worlds is so thin that the spirits of the dead can cross over into the world of the living and communication with them is easier. It is also the time when the malicious spirits of the Little People come out of hiding. In the ancient Irish tradition of Jack o'Lantern (from an Irish fairy tale), turnips were carved with terrifying faces and candles placed inside to scare away the spirits. Later, turnips were swapped for pumpkins because they were easier to hollow out. In Celtic druid tradition, terrifying masks were worn to ward off evil creatures.

This celebration aims to commemorate the cycles of life. It marks the start of the dark season and symbolizes self-work, introspection and wisdom. It is also one of the three nights of the spirits, during which we make prophecies.

Associations

Planet	Pluto
Elements	Water, fire
Deities	Hecate, Osiris, Morrigan, Demeter, Isis
Plants	Sage, mint, cypress, marigold, chrysanthemum, clove
Crystals	Carnelian, onyx, obsidian, amber
Colours	Orange, black, purple

Decorating the altar

At Samhain, the altar is traditionally decorated with a black cloth, along with seasonal fruits and vegetables, autumn flowers, and photos of our ancestors.

Cloth	Black
Candles	Red, orange, white
Tools	Cauldron, broom
Symbols	Mask, skull, spider, crow
Plants	Chrysanthemum, marigold, pine cone, rosemary, cedar

The Samhain ritual

The energies of Samhain are perfect for divination and for performing banishment, healing and purification rituals, to cast off the negative aspects of our lives and heal our wounds.

MATERIALS: paper, pen, matches, tarot or oracle

1. Once you have set up your altar and lit the candles, position yourself, open your notebook, and take a few moments to draw a tree symbolizing yourself.

2. Start with the roots, which represent your past and your ancestors, then draw the trunk to represent your personality and your inner world. Continue with the branches to symbolize your beliefs, the leaves to represent your emotions, and the fruits which represent your achievements.

3. Write the name of your ancestors on the roots, the way in which you perceive yourself on the trunk, your beliefs of the world on the leaves, and your achievements over the past year on the fruits.

4. Take the time to look at, admire and contemplate your tree, and meditate on its representation. Next, cut out the parts of the tree that you wish to change or that you wish to discard, visualize them and burn them.

5. Take out your tarot or oracle cards and draw three cards. The first represents what you must avoid in the future, the second what is to come in the months ahead, and the third what you should focus on. Look at them, interpret them and note down your analysis.

The esbats of the full moon

The phases of the moon

The moon passes through the zodiac in about 28 days. This lunar cycle, also called lunation, is divided into eight phases which symbolize biological rhythms, fecundity, periodic renewal, time, cyclical rebirth, night, dreams, and the unconscious.

New moon

The new moon occurs when the moon, the sun and the earth are aligned and symbolizes renewal. The energies of the new moon give us the opportunity to call on ourselves, on our intuition, and on our hearts. This phase doesn't really benefit magic, so perform rituals that do not call on the energies at this time.

Waxing crescent

During this phase, the moon becomes more visible and its power of attraction is perfect for performing rituals associated with change, healing, luck, wealth and love.

First quarter

The moon is half full; its energies are powerful, and this is a time for action. It symbolizes creativity, force and desire. It is a good time to perform divination rituals.

Waxing gibbous moon

This the last phase before the full moon. It is a symbol of success, prosperity and luck, which gives us greater stability. It is a good time to perform rituals concerning relationships and communication.

Twelve or Thirteen moons?

Pagans and Wiccans celebrate the esbats, or full moons. Depending on the year, there are 12 or 13 full moons. When the first full moon of January occurs between 1st and 11th January, there will be 13 full moons in the year, otherwise there will only be 12.

Full moon

The moon is at its largest now, and its powerful energies are perfect for practising magic. This period is the time to perform rituals associated with divination, dreams and clairvoyance. It symbolizes achievement, balance, harmony, healing, purification and love.

Waning gibbous moon

The moon loses some of its intensity. Its energies make this a good time to perform banishing, purifying and cleansing rituals, to rid ourselves of negative influences.

Third quarter

This phase of the moon symbolizes awareness. It is a time for putting things in order and for introspection.

Waning crescent

One cycle is ending and a new one is beginning. With it comes a sense of balance. This phase is not recommended for magic. It symbolizes success, wisdom, forgiveness and healing.

Associations

Principle	Feminine, yin
Sign	Cancer
Element	Water
Deities	Hecate, Isis, Artemis-Diana, Ishtar, Selene, Virgin Mary
Crystals	Moonstone, selenite, quartz
Colour	White

The moon and the zodiac

Each full moon brings new energies as the moon passes through the zodiac signs.

Aries: First sign of the zodiac, Aries corresponds with the strengthening sun, the transition from dark to light and from cool to warm. It symbolizes the awakening of the world and humankind, and marks the first impulse of the big bang that created the universe. Its energies during the full moon call for us to let go of the past and to commune with the All.

Taurus: Second sign of the zodiac, Taurus lies between the spring equinox and the summer solstice. It symbolizes instinct, sensuality, generosity and vitality. Its energies during the full moon call for us to open ourselves to the world and listen to our intuition.

Gemini: Third sign of the zodiac, Gemini symbolizes duality, the opposite and the complementary, the relative and the absolute. It highlights the polarity between the spiritual and the physical. It represents opposites such as masculine and feminine, dark and light. Its energies during the full moon call for us to create a creative ambiance and return to our true values.

Cancer: Fourth sign of the zodiac, Cancer marks a change in the sun's direction from ascending to descending. It is a symbol of the original water and the nurturing principle. It symbolizes sensitivity, tenacity, shyness, dreams, the imagination, mediation and mediumship.

114

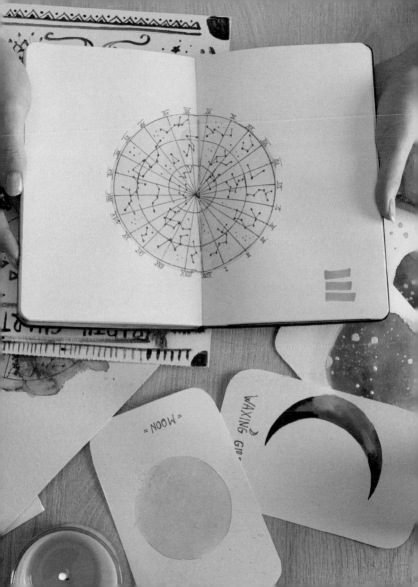

Leo: Fifth sign of the zodiac, Leo embodies the fulfilment of nature, elevation, ambition, the joy of life, pride and strength, warmth, power and light. Its energies during the full moon call for us to take stock of our feelings and to accept them and our situation. They bring new perspectives.

Virgo: Sixth sign of the zodiac, Virgo symbolizes harvests, work, precision and dexterity, and enshrines differences. Its energies during the full moon call for us to share our feelings to purify ourselves and to regain self-confidence.

Libra: Seventh sign of the zodiac, Libra reflects the balance between day and night. The sun's passage from the Northern Hemisphere to the Southern Hemisphere indicates that it is at its median point in the astronomical year. It symbolizes sociability, harmonization and transformation. Its energies during the full moon call for us to cast off our illusions so that we can take action.

Scorpio: Eighth sign of the zodiac, Scorpio symbolizes resistance, vitality, endurance and struggle. It evokes the chaos of matter before the rebirth of life. Its energies during the full moon call for us to synchronize with the earth and our deeper nature.

Sagittarius: Ninth sign of the zodiac, Sagittarius symbolizes movement, independence and the duality of instinct and higher aspirations, humankind's return to God. Its energies during the full moon call for us to pour out our love on the world, and to demonstrate kindness and compassion.

Capricorn: Tenth sign of the zodiac, Capricorn starts at the winter solstice. It represents the elevation, or the death of the physical universe, and corresponds with spiritual fulfilment. It represents the end of one cycle and the start of a new one. It symbolizes caution, patience, perseverance and achievement. Its energies during the full moon call for us to overcome difficulties, draw on our inner strength and meditate on our objectives.

Aquarius: Eleventh sign of the zodiac, Aquarius marks the transition to states of higher consciousness, and symbolizes fraternity, cooperation, solidarity and letting go of material things. Its energies during the full moon call for us to consider new opportunities, to put all our energy into everything we do, and to express our love and creativity.

Pisces: Twelfth and last sign of the zodiac, Pisces marks the spring equinox. It symbolizes the psyche and the inner world, or the transition to initial oneness. Its energies call for us to restore balance and stability, but also to follow our deeper aspirations.

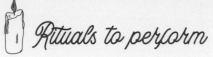

Rituals to perform

The full moon marks a moment of achievement and mental openness during which we express gratitude. Many rituals can be performed at this time.

How to perform rituals

Generally, we start by opening a circle. After a moment of meditation, we perform the ritual, and then finish with a card reading (oracle or tarot) before closing the circle.

TOOLS: tarot, oracle, notebook, pencil

ALTAR: white candles, offering bowl, crystals, plants

Ritual steps

1. Cast the circle
2. Meditation
3. Ritual
4. Card reading
5. Close the circle

January full moon

The January full moon is the Wolf Moon, or Winter Moon. It symbolizes strength and calls for us to perform a protection ritual, and to organize our new projects.

MATERIAL: paper or notebook, pencil, tarot or oracle, bag or vial (protection), wormwood, angelica, mugwort

1. Set up your altar, light your candle, then cast your circle and call on the elements, the moon, the cardinal directions, your guides, and the divinities of your choosing. Take the time to look at the moon or visualize it.

2. Sit down, breathe, and meditate on your connection with the moon. Show gratitude for its energies, and for what it symbolizes.

3. Note down on a piece of paper how you have felt in recent days, as well as anything you thought about during your meditation. Then write down your new projects, the new objectives you would like to achieve.

4. Take your cards and draw three. The first will symbolize what you must acknowledge and accept, the second what you must focus on, and the third what is to come in the weeks ahead.

5. You can make a bag or vial to provide you with protection. Purify your container with a smudge stick or incense, then place the wormwood, angelica and mugwort inside.

6. Thank the elements, the divinities, the moon and all you have called on, then close the circle.

February full moon

The February full moon is the Storm Moon, or the Moon of the Dead, which symbolizes force and renewal. It calls for us to perform a purification ritual to rid ourselves of any negativity in our lives.

MATERIAL: paper or notebook, pencil, tarot or oracle, Epsom salts, chamomile, lavender

1. Set up your celebration space and light your candle. Cast your circle and take a few moments to admire the moon and visualize the elements.

2. Allow yourself a moment to meditate, relax your body and express your emotions. Think about the energies of the moon and let them surround you. Have confidence.

3. On a piece of paper or in your notebook, write down everything you would like to offload. This may be feelings, beliefs, people, or situations. Write down all the negative aspects that you want to cast off.

4. Burn the piece of paper whilst you visualize each word disappearing.

5. Take out your tarot or oracle cards and draw three. The first will symbolize what you must offload, the second what you must talk about, and the third what you must do to develop.

5. You can take a salt bath to purify yourself, using 3 parts Epsom salts, 1 part chamomile and 1 part lavender.

6. To finish this ritual, thank all you have called on, then close the circle.

March full moon

March's full moon is the Chaste Moon, or Worm Moon, which symbolizes hope and success. It is the ideal time for performing a blessing ritual and to start carrying out the projects you noted during January's full moon.

MATERIAL: paper or notebook, pencil, tarot or oracle, seeds and objects to bless

1. Once you have set up your altar and lit your candle, cast your circle and call on the elements, the cardinal directions, and your guides or the divinities of your choosing.

2. Meditate on your connection with the moon and express your feelings, without judgement.

3. Take the list of projects set out during January's full moon and identify what you have already done to implement them and what remains to be done to achieve them.

4. Take out your cards and draw three. The first will symbolize the illusions that prevent you from making progress and that you must set aside, the second what lies ahead in the coming weeks, and the third what you must do to take action.

5. Say the following to bless your projects, your objects or your seeds:

"I bless this [name of the seed or object] by
fire, water, earth and air.
So may it be."

6. To finish this ritual, thank all you have called on, then close the circle.

April full moon

The April full moon is the Seed Moon, or Egg Moon, which symbolizes fertility and growth. It calls for us to perform a ritual for earthly growth, and for taking action.

MATERIAL: paper or notebook, pencil

1. Set up your altar with crystals, an offering bowl, and your candle, which you can then light. Cast your circle and invite the elements, the moon, the cardinal directions, and your guides.

2. Take time to contemplate the moon or visualize it, then meditate on the earth, your connection with it, as well as on your deepest nature.

3. When you have finished meditating, make a gratitude list that you can read to the moon, to the divinities, to the universe, to your guides and to all the energies or beings you wish to thank.

4. You can also use cards to bring clarity. Draw three cards. The first will symbolize what you must offload, the second what will bring you light, and the third what will bring about your rebirth.

5. Ask the divinities, the elements, the cardinal directions, the universe to bring their favours, their blessings and their strength to your projects, to your crops or anything else of your choosing.

6. To end the ritual, thank the elements, the divinities, the moon and all you have called on, then close the circle.

May full moon

May's full moon is the Hare Moon or the Flower Moon, which symbolizes love, romance and health. It is the perfect time to perform a love ritual.

MATERIAL: paper or notebook, pencil, tarot or oracle, bag, yarrow, cedar, rosemary

1. Once your altar to love is set up and you have lit your candle, cast your circle and take a moment to meditate on your connection with the moon, with love and gentleness.

2. Take your cards and draw three. The first will symbolize your emotions, the second how you must express your love, and the third the romance you are interested in.

3. You can create a love charm bag using the rosemary, yarrow and cedar.

4. To finish this ritual, thank all you have called on, then close the circle.

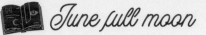

June full moon

June's full moon is the Love Moon, or the Rose Moon, which symbolizes energy and success. It is the perfect time to perform a strength ritual.

MATERIAL: paper or notebook, pencil, tarot or oracle

1. Set up your altar with crystals, an offering bowl, and your candle, which you will then light, then cast your circle.

2. Take the time to contemplate the moon and absorb its energies before meditating on the energy and force that lies within you.

3. When you have finished your meditation, write down a list of the difficulties you are facing, then a list of all the things you can do to overcome them.

4. Take out your cards and draw three. The first will symbolize what you must offload, the second what will bring you force, and the third what awaits you.

5. Say a prayer to get strength:

> *"I call on the elements, on my guides...*
> *To give me the strength to overcome the*
> *difficulties that obstruct my path."*

6. Ask the divinities, the elements, the cardinal directions, the universe to bring their favours, their blessings and their strength to your projects, to your crops or anything else of your choosing.

7. Thank the elements, the divinities, the moon and all you have called on, then close the circle.

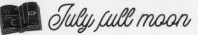 July full moon

July's full moon is the Prairie Moon, or the Blessing Moon, which symbolizes renewal and success. It is the perfect time to carry out a prosperity ritual and to perform magic.

MATERIAL: paper or notebook, pencil, matches, tarot or oracle, lemon balm, clove, coins, bag

1. Set up your altar with crystals, an offering bowl, and your lit candle. Cast your circle and invite the elements, the moon, the cardinal directions, and your guides.

2. Take the time to contemplate the moon or visualize it before meditating on your connection with the moon.

3. When you have finished your meditation, write a list of all the opportunities that are open to you.

4. Draw three cards to bring you clarity. The first will symbolize what life offers you, the second what you must do to achieve it, and the third renewal.

5. You can make a charm bag to achieve success, in which you place the lemon balm, cloves and a few coins.

6. To end the ritual, thank the elements, the divinities, the moon and all you have called on, then close the circle.

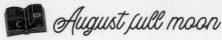 *August full moon*

The August full moon is the Herb Moon, or Barley Moon, which symbolizes the abundance of crops. It calls for us to perform an abundance ritual.

MATERIAL: paper or notebook, pencil, tarot or oracle

1. Set up your celebration space with your crystals, a candle, and an offering bowl, then light your candle. Cast your circle and take a few moments to admire the moon or visualize it.

2. Allow yourself a moment to meditate, relax your body and express your emotions. Think about the energies of the moon and let them surround you. Have confidence.

3. On a piece of paper or in your notebook, draw your representation of the love that you feel for yourself, for others and for the moon. Then take the time to admire your drawing.

4. Take out your tarot or oracle cards and draw three. The first will symbolize what you should get rid of, the second what you should focus on, and the third what is to come in the weeks ahead.

5. You can say a few words of thanks to the moon:

*"Thank you for the abundance
you bring to my life."*

6. To finish this ritual, thank all you have called on, then close the circle.

September full moon

September's full moon is the Harvest Moon, or Hunter's Moon, which symbolizes protection, abundance and prosperity. It is the perfect time to perform a healing ritual to bring balance.

MATERIAL: paper or notebook, pencil, tarot or oracle, Epsom salts, cinnamon, angelica

1. Set up your celebration space with your crystals, a candle, and an offering bowl. Light your candle and cast your circle.

2. Allow yourself a moment to meditate, relax your body and express your emotions Think about the energies of the moon and let them surround you. Have confidence.

3. On a piece of paper or in your notebook, write down what you really desire, your deepest aspirations.

4. Take out your tarot or oracle cards and draw three. The first will symbolize what you must get rid of, the second what you must share, and the third what you must do to develop.

5. You can take a healing salt bath using Epsom salts, angelica and cinnamon.

6. To finish this ritual, thank all you have called on, then close the circle.

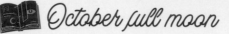 *October full moon*

October's full moon is the Blood Moon, or Leaf Moon, which symbolizes resolution and spirituality. It is the perfect time to perform introspection and divination rituals.

MATERIAL: paper or notebook, pencil, objects, divination tools (tarot, oracle, pendulum, etc.), divination incense

1. Set up your celebration space with your crystals, a candle, and an offering bowl. Light your candle and cast your circle, then take a few moments to admire the moon or visualize it.

2. Take a moment to meditate on your deepest nature and visit your consciousness.

3. On a piece of paper or in your notebook, write down everything that is weighing you down, the things that you would like to offload, then burn it as you visualise it disappearing.

4. The energies of this full moon are perfect for divination. It is the ideal moment to take out your divination objects and practise using them. To help you, you can create a divination incense (see page 150).

5. To finish this ritual, thank all you have called on, then close the circle.

November full moon

November's full moon is the Snow Moon, or the Mourning Moon, which symbolizes family bonds. It is the perfect time to perform a grounding ritual.

MATERIAL: paper or notebook, pencil, tarot or oracle, incense or smudge stick

1. Once you have set up your altar and cast your circle, take a moment to meditate, express your emotions, open your heart to the world and listen to your feelings and your intuition. Ground yourself.

2. On a piece of paper or in your notebook, write down a list of the obstacles that you may have encountered and then burn the piece of paper while you visualize each word disappearing.

3. Take out your tarot or oracle cards and draw three. The first will symbolize what you must get rid of, the second what you must share, and the third what you must do to develop.

4. To finish this ritual, thank all you have called on, then close the circle.

December full moon

December's full moon is the Oak Moon, or Cold Moon, which symbolizes hope and change. It is the perfect time to perform a healing ritual.

MATERIAL: paper or notebook, pencil, tarot or oracle, pine resin, sage, mint

1. Set up your celebration space with your crystals, a candle, and an offering bowl. Light your candle and cast your circle, then take a few moments to admire the moon or visualize it.

2. Allow yourself a moment to meditate, relax your body and express your emotions. Think about the energies of the moon and let them surround you. Have confidence.

3. On a piece of paper or in your notebook, write down everything you would like to offload. This may be feelings, beliefs, people, or situations. Write down all the negative aspects that you want to cast off. Burn the piece of paper while visualizing each word on the list disappearing.

4. Take out your tarot or oracle cards and draw three. The first will symbolize what you must get rid of, the second what is to come in the weeks ahead, and the third what you must undertake.

5. You can make a healing incense using the pine resin, sage and mint.

6. To finish this ritual, thank all you have called on, then close the circle.

In the Wicca workshop

Moon water

Moon water is charged with the energies of the moon and has many beneficial properties, determined by which phase the moon was in when the water was made (see pages 110–113).

Making your own moon water

1. Find a container made of a natural material (clay, glass, etc.).

2. Fill it with spring water, rainwater or dew.

3. You can add plants and crystals depending on the powers you wish to give your water (see page 149).

4. Place the container outside at moon rise and leave until moon set.

5. When you collect your water, thank the moon, then pour the water into a bottle.

When to use moon water

As well as being used for rituals, moon water can be used in cooking or as a drink to allow you to absorb its benefits. It can also be used for making cosmetics, watering your plants, taking a lunar bath, and cleaning your crystals and divination tools.

Powers	Plants	Crystals
Love	Wormwood, yarrow, lady's mantle, basil, cherry tree, hemp, coriander, hibiscus, jasmine, lavender, lemon balm	Rose quartz, rhodocrosite, kunzite, rubelite, morganite
Protection	Wormwood, agrimony, dill, angelica, burdock, basil, sandalwood, cedar, thistle, clove, cumin, fennel, juniper, lavender, ivy, lilac, mint, myrrh	Tourmaline, black obsidian, celestial eye obsidian, brimstone, tiger eye, falcon eye
Purification	Aniseed, benzoin, chamomile, cedar, copal, turmeric, fennel, hyssop, iris, bay, mimosa, parsley	Quartz, tourmaline, salt
Divination	Cherry tree, hibiscus, corn, mallow, St John's wort, mullein, periwinkle	Seraphinite, apophyllite, cyanite, clear calcite, moldavite
Prosperity	Dill, benzoin, chamomile, clove, ginger, jasmine, flax	Citrine, jade, pyrite, moss agate, aventurine
Fertility	Lady's mantle, hawthorn, wheat, fern, daffodil, patchouli, poppy	Adularia moonstone, peristerite, rose quartz, unakite
Healing	Burdock, sandalwood, hemp, thistle, coriander, common hop, ivy, lemon balm, mint, myrrh, marigold	Chrysocolla, turquoise, aquamarine, chrysoprase, peridot

Incense

The symbolic aspect of incense comes from its smoke, its fragrance, and the plants used to make it. Universally used by many societies, such as the Mayans, the Egyptians, the American Indians, and Christians, it symbolizes the bond between humankind and the divine during ceremonies. In Celtic tradition, it was believed that the smoke of funeral pyres carried away the souls of the dead.

Making incense

Depending on the plants and resins used in its creation, incense has many benefits: it purifies, protects, aids sleep, induces dreams, stimulates mediumnic activity, and promotes positive energy during meditation.

1. In a mortar, crush your chosen dried plants and resin into a powder.

2. Pour the mix into a vial and label it with the date, its use and the ingredients.

3. Store the vial in a cool, dark place.

4. When you wish to use it, place some of the mixture in a heat-resistant container over red hot charcoal.

Safety precautions

Always burn incense in a well-ventilated room. Keep away from children and animals.

150

Incense recipes

The ingredients in each recipe should be mixed together in equal parts. The plants used here are all dried.

- **Divination incense:** mugwort, sandalwood, fennel, poppy seeds, iris root

- **Protection incense:** agrimony, angelica, burdock, pine resin, violet

- **Purification incense:** benzoin, chamomile, cedar, thyme

- **Moon incense:** benzoin, common poppy, poppy seeds, linden tree

151

Oils

Oils are mainly used during rituals as an incense, or to cast symbols. Note, these oils are not to be consumed or used on the body!

Making magic oil

There are two ways to assess the quantity of plants needed to make a macerated oil:
• Either fill a bowl with flowers to the top, compact them down, then cover with vegetable oil (olive oil, sunflower, jojoba, etc.).
• Or use one part flowers to ten parts oil (e.g. 20g/³⁄₄oz of flowers with 200g/7oz of oil).

1. Crush the plants with a pestle and then place them in a glass jar.

2. Cover them with the oil, then seal the jar tightly.

3. Leave to macerate (using the hot or cold method, see opposite).

4. Filter the oil using a clean muslin cloth, then with a coffee filter.

5. Pour the oil into an opaque glass vial and label it with the date and ingredients. Store the vial in a cool, dark place.

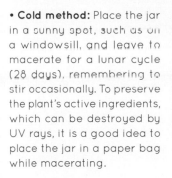

• **Cold method:** Place the jar in a sunny spot, such as on a windowsill, and leave to macerate for a lunar cycle (28 days), remembering to stir occasionally. To preserve the plant's active ingredients, which can be destroyed by UV rays, it is a good idea to place the jar in a paper bag while macerating.

Witch's secret

You can add vitamin E to the oil (approximately 2 drops to every 100g/3½oz) if liked.

• **Hot method:** Place the jar in a bain-marie over a gentle heat and leave to simmer for two hours. Turn off the heat and leave to rest for one hour in the warm water.

Magic oil recipes

Pour the oil into a heat-resistant container over a tea light warmer, or place a few drops onto a hot coal in a cauldron.

- **Samhain oil:** olive oil, cinnamon, pine needles, sage
- **Yule oil:** olive oil, ivy, rosemary, red rose
- **Imbolc oil:** olive oil, basil, frankincense, snowdrop
- **Ostara oil:** olive oil, honeysuckle, willow, violet
- **Beltane oil:** olive oil, hawthorn, jasmine, lilac
- **Litha oil:** olive oil, oak wood, St John's wort, sage
- **Lughnasadh oil:** olive oil, willow wood, hazel leaves, wheat grains
- **Mabon oil:** olive oil, sandalwood, marigold, sage

- **Water oil:** olive oil, chamomile, passion flower, wild pansy
- **Earth oil:** olive oil, honeysuckle, barberry, plantain
- **Air oil:** olive oil, borage, common hops, lavender
- **Fire oil:** olive oil, hawthorn, hyssop, bay laurel
- **Moon oil:** olive oil, sandalwood, camphor, jasmine

Magic candles

To make a magic candle, first decide on its colour (see pages 42–45), then engrave it with symbols such as runes, sigils, the elements (earth, air, water, fire), a cross, a star, or a moon.

The sigil

Sigil means "seal", a geometric symbol that is created using a combination of letters, geometric forms, or symbols associated with divinities, alchemy or astrology, for example. Used since the dawn of time by wizards, witches and alchemists, it can be drawn on any kind of medium (paper, window, body, etc.) to represent an intention.

There are many ways to make a sigil, but the most common is shown below:

1. Your statement of intent is: "I am protected." To keep the statement as short as possible, remove any duplicate letters and the vowels: "MPRTCD".

2. On a sigil wheel or rose (drawing above), link the letters to form a symbol).

3. Copy your symbol onto the medium of your choice. To activate the symbol, concentrate all your focus on your intention, either by looking at the sigil, or by visualizing it as you meditate.

Runes

Fehu	ᚠ	Rune associated with fire, it symbolizes movement, change, transformation, strength, health, abundance and prosperity.
Uruz	ᚢ	The rune of primal strength, it symbolizes gestation, birth and protection.
Thurisaz	ᚦ	Rune of strength and power, it symbolizes the capacity to overcome.
Ansuz	ᚨ	Rune of the Aesir, it symbolizes wisdom, intelligence, inspiration, knowledge, magic, the word and communication.
Raidho	ᚱ	Rune of the chariot, the path and the wheel, it represents the inner and earthly journey, development, energy, growth, order and rules.
Kenaz	ᚲ	Rune of fire, it symbolizes momentum, light, transformation, liberty, purification and the ability to control energy.
Gebo	ᚷ	Rune of the interaction between two forces, two energies, it symbolizes affection, love, generosity, union and sharing.
Wunjo	ᚹ	Symbolizes harmony, joy, happiness and togetherness.
Hagalaz	ᚺ	Symbolizes danger, life, positive change, duality and destiny.
Naudhiz	ᚾ	Associated with the sacrificial fire, it symbolizes crises, challenges and changes of course.
Isa	ᛁ	Powerful rune of ice, it symbolizes will, perseverance, and the return to the earth, to the physical world and to unity.
Jera	ᛃ	Symbolizes the summer harvests, well-earned rewards (we reap what we sow), success, joy and happiness.

Eihwaz	ᛇ	A protective rune, it is associated with the symbol of the sacred tree, hidden influences, mystery, the occult and communication between worlds.
Perthor	ᛈ	Symbolizes chance, destiny, divination, spiritual birth, development and growing consciousness.
Algiz	ᛉ	Meaning "elk", nurturing animal, protective force, it symbolizes communication with the divine and represents the protective spirits of the warriors.
Sowilo	ᛋ	Meaning "sun", it symbolizes the solar wheel, success, liberation, power, illumination, thunder, light, force and prosperity.
Tiwaz	ᛏ	Rune of the god of war, order and justice (Tyr), it symbolizes commitment, responsibility, combat, will and courage.
Berkano	ᛒ	Meaning "birth", it symbolizes the Mother Goddess, birth, the cycles of life, death and rebirth.
Ehwaz	ᛖ	Rune of duality and complementarity, it symbolizes reunification, mobility, adventure, discovery and spiritual journey.
Mannaz	ᛗ	Symbolizes everything to do with humankind, the mind, the masses, spirituality and mutual support between humans.
Laguz	ᛚ	Symbolizes the water of life, positive energies, good health, intuition, vitality, change, renewal and adaptation.
Ingwaz	ᛜ	Rune of the god of fecundity, fertility and nature, it symbolizes creativity, germination, new projects and love.
Dagaz	ᛞ	Rune of the day, it symbolizes achievement, awareness, awakening, lucidity, light and balance.
Othala	ᛟ	Symbolizes karmic heritage, spiritual legacies and customs.

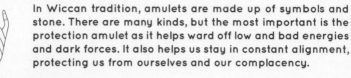

Protection amulet

In Wiccan tradition, amulets are made up of symbols and stone. There are many kinds, but the most important is the protection amulet as it helps ward off low and bad energies and dark forces. It also helps us stay in constant alignment, protecting us from ourselves and our complacency.

Symbols

OGHAMS

Ogham script is an ancient alphabet mainly used to write primitive Irish. It was also the sacred writing of the druids. It originally had twenty letters divided into four groups of five letters. Another group of five letters was added at a later date. They are traditionally engraved like notches.

TRISKELION

This Celtic symbol represents a wheel with three legs around its centre. Each of the legs represent water, air and fire, respectively. At the centre is the earth. This symbol represents the eternal renewal of life. The triskelion is traditionally dextrorotating, which means that it turns in a clockwise direction.

TRIPLE MOON

Also called the Triple Goddess, the triple moon has several levels of representation:

- **The three stages of a woman's life:** maiden, mother and old woman.
- **The three planes of existence:** the underworld, the earth and the heavens.
- **The three phases of human existence:** birth, life and death.
- **The three periods of the soul's journey:** the before, the during and the after.

It also symbolizes creation, maternity, sexuality, sensuality and the magic of the Goddess. The goddess Hecate and her three heads is represented by the triple moon.

The triquetra

In latin, *triquetra* means "three elbows". It consists of three intertwined loops, creating the intersection of three circles. It is a variant of the symbol of the triple moon: maid, mother and old woman.

Stones

NATIVE SULPHUR

This is a stone with an orthorhombic crystal structure. Often associated with the underworld because of its odour, sulphur is in fact an excellent protection stone. It's extremely brittle and is soluble in water.

TOURMALINE

This is a black stone with a rhombohedral crystal structure. It is the most well-known protection stone. It represents grounding and will protect you from low energies and electromagnetic pollution.

ROCK CRYSTAL

Also known as quartz, rock crystal is a stone with a rhombohedral crystal structure, like tourmaline. It is not designed to protect, but you can dedicate it for this. Use the consecration ritual (page 70), saying to each element: "Let this stone be dedicated to my protection".

Making an amulet

You can buy protection amulets but it is better to make your own.

MATERIAL: air-dry clay, string, a stone of your choosing, some cocktail sticks

1. Roll out the clay to a thickness of 3mm (⅛in), and cut out a peanut shape measuring about 10cm (4in).

2. Place your stone at the bottom of the clay shape, half on and half off the clay.

3. Place six cocktail sticks across the narrowest part of the peanut and fold the upper part over the lower part. Your amulet should resemble a full moon with a small stone poking out the bottom.

4. With your fingers, press down the edges of the clay around the stone.

5. Using a cocktail stick, draw your symbol on the amulet, then leave it in a dry, dark place for 24 hours.

Witchcraft tip

If you decide to use sulphur for your amulet, encase it in two layers of clay.

6. When the clay has dried, remove the cocktail sticks. Thread string through the space left by the sticks to make a necklace.

7. If you like, paint and varnish your amulet, then consecrate it (page 70).

Sabbat recipes

Yule ✦
REBIRTHING LOG

The Yule log is one of the most important emblems of this sabbat because it represents the rebirth of the sun. Take great care when making this delicious wintry cake and share it with family or in the coven to celebrate the return of the light.

INGREDIENTS: 250g (9oz) sugar, 200g (7oz) butter, 4 eggs, 400g (14oz) flour, 1 sachet of yeast, 1 teaspoon orange powder, 80ml (⅓ cup) milk, 3 tablespoons cocoa powder

1. Beat the butter and sugar until the mixture is fluffy and light, then add the eggs one by one.

2. In a separate bowl, mix the flour, yeast and orange powder, then incorporate the dry mixture into the egg mixture.

3. Slowly add 70 ml (¼ cup) of milk and mix well until smooth.

4. Divide the mixture between two bowls.

5. Add the cocoa powder and remaining milk to one of the bowls and beat together. You now have two mixtures, one light and the other dark, representing the battle between light and dark at Yule.

6. Pour the cocoa mixture into the light mixture, saying: "Blessed be the sun's return."

7. With the handle of a spoon, stir briefly (no more than 2 or 3 times) to draw stripes in the batter.

8. Pour the batter into a buttered and floured bread tin and bake at 180°C (350°F) for 1 hour.

9. When the log has cooled, take it out of the tin, sprinkle it with icing sugar and decorate with orange slices and chocolate!

Imbolc ✦ VIOLET AND LEMON MOON CRESCENTS

These crescent-shaped moon biscuits represent the end of winter and the dark, the awakening of the earth and the Mother Goddess.

INGREDIENTS: 70g (2½oz) softened butter, 70g (2½oz) ground almonds, 50g (1¾oz) brown sugar, 20g (¾oz) candied violets, 1 egg, zest of 1 lemon, 100g (3½oz) flour, 20g (¾oz) almond flakes

1. In a bowl, mix the butter, ground almonds and sugar. Beat together until creamy.

2. Add the violets and lemon zest then gently incorporate the egg.

3. Mix in the flour and almond flakes, shape the mixture into a ball and place it in the fridge for at least 1 hour.

4. Once cooled and hardened, roll the ball into a 3-cm (1¼-in) thick sausage.

5. Using a knife, cut 8-cm (3¼-in.) segments and shape them into crescents.

6. Bake for at 180°C (350°F) for 10 minutes.

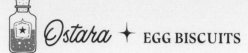

Ostara ✦ EGG BISCUITS

Ostara has become the traditional Easter holiday, with chocolate rabbits and egg hunts. The rabbit is an ancient symbol of the moon, which represents the renewal of the earth's fertility. The full-moon shape of these biscuits represents the rounded stomach of the Mother Goddess, the eggs symbolize fertility, and their light golden colour symbolizes the God who enables life.

INGREDIENTS: 80g (2¾oz) butter, 2 egg yolks, 100g (3½oz) sugar, 100g (3½oz) flour, 100g (3½oz) ground hazelnuts

1. Melt the butter and leave it to cool.

2. Meanwhile, beat the egg yolks with the sugar until pale, then add the melted butter.

3. Mix in the flour and ground hazelnuts.

4. Shape the dough into small balls and place them on a baking tray covered with baking paper, leaving space between them.

5. Bake at 180°C (350°F) for 8 to 10 min, until they start to turn golden (keep an eye on them to ensure they don't burn).

 *Beltane* ✦ MAY WINE

Beltane is a wonderful opportunity to honour the living and celebrate being together. Welcome spring by enjoying a glass of wine with friends and family at this special time.

INGREDIENTS: 1 litre (4⅓ cups) organic white wine, 2 tablespoons brown sugar, 20 stems fresh sweet woodruff

1. Pour the wine into a large jar.

2. Add the sugar and whole sweet woodruff.

3. Close the jar tightly and leave to macerate from the first quarter moon of May until the new moon.

4. Filter and bottle the wine. Your wine will be slightly sparkling from the fermentation process.

Witch's secret

Sweet woodruff, also known as sweet-scented bedstraw, is used to calm anxiety, stress, vertigo and palpitations.

Litha ✦ ROSE, STRAWBERRY AND THYME TART

For the summer solstice, here is a refreshing recipe that honours nature.

FOR THE CRÈME PÂTISSIÈRE: 250ml (generous 1 cup) milk, 2 egg yolks, 20g (¾oz) sugar, 2 tablespoons cornflour, 1 tablespoon rose water

FOR THE PASTRY: 150g (5½oz) butter, 30g (1oz) ground almonds 1 egg, 200g (7oz) flour, 1 pinch salt, 50g (1¾oz) icing sugar

FOR THE FILLING: 1 punnet organic strawberries, 1 sprig fresh thyme, 1 small handful of dried rosebuds

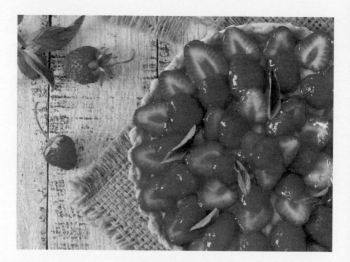

1. Place all the pastry ingredients in a bowl and knead until the pastry is smooth but still a little crumbly. Cover with a cloth and leave to rest in the refrigerator for 1 hour.

2. Bring the milk for the crème pâtissière to a simmer (but do not boil).

3. Beat the egg yolks with the sugar and cornflour, then gradually whisk in the warm milk.

4. Pour the mixture back into the pan over a low heat and stir continuously until the mixture thickens.

5. Add the rose water, cover with cling film and leave to cool.

6. Remove the pastry from the refrigerator and spread over the bottom of a lined tart dish.

7. Cook in a pre-heated oven at 180°C (350°F) for 15 minutes.

8. When the pastry crust has cooled, pour in the crème pâtissière, then fill with pieces of strawberry.

9. Add the thyme sprigs with their leaves removed, and the rosebud petals.

Lughnasadh ✦
WHEAT AND CORN BREAD

This is the time of year when life is at its peak. It is time to celebrate wheat, gold and light, and the promises of life by breaking bread together.

INGREDIENTS: 40g (1½oz) fresh yeast, 100g (3½oz) polenta, 500g (1lb 2oz) wheat flour, 180ml (¾cup) warm water, 1 pinch salt, 1 tablespoon honey

1. Dilute the yeast in a little warm water. In a bowl, mix together the polenta, flour and yeast.

2. Make a small well in the centre and pour in the warm water, salt and honey.

3. Mix and knead until the dough is smooth.

4. Cover with a tea towel (dish towel) and leave to rise for 1 ½ hours.

5. Remove the air bubbles from the dough by kneading briefly, shape into a ball and leave to rise for 40 minutes.

6. Shape your bread and cut notches on the top, then place in a cold oven and bake at 220°C (430°F) for 45 minutes. Remember to place a small bowl of water in the oven while baking to keep the bread moist.

Mabon ✦
APPLE AND CHESTNUT JAM

Mabon is a time of abundance and celebration of the harvests. We also prepare for winter at this time, and what could be better than making pots of jam to be enjoyed throughout the cold months ahead?

INGREDIENTS: 600g (1lb 5oz) chestnuts, 1kg (2lb 4oz) apples, 1 vanilla pod, 800g (1lb 12oz) sugar, 150ml (scant ⅔ cup) water

1. Score the skin of the chestnuts deep enough to cut through the inner skin.

2. Bring a large pan of water to the boil, then lower the heat and cook a handful of chestnuts for 5 minutes.

3. Remove the chestnuts, cool in cold water and quickly remove the skin with your fingers.

4. Repeat until all the chestnuts are boiled and peeled, and then roast for 15 minutes.

5. Meanwhile, peel, core and quarter the apples.

6. Cover the bottom of a frying pan with water, add the vanilla pod and the chestnuts and cook over a low heat for 15 minutes.

7. Blend the chestnuts, apples, sugar and 150ml (scant ⅔cup) of water together until chunky and not too smooth.

8. Boil again until large bubbles form, then pour into sterilized jam jars.

9. Seal the jars and store in a cool, dark place.

Samhain ✦

PUMPKIN AND SPICE CAKE

Samhain marks the end of the harvests and the beginning of the darkest, coldest season of the year. Pumpkin celebrates the harvests and the spices bring some warmth for the cold months ahead.

INGREDIENTS: 4 eggs, 175g (6oz) brown sugar, 175g (6oz) ground almonds, 75g (2½oz) flour, 2½ teaspoons baking powder, 1 tablespoon ground cinnamon, ½ teaspoon ground ginger, ½ teaspoon ground nutmeg, 2 ground cloves, 250g (9oz) grated pumpkin

1. In a large bowl, beat the eggs and brown sugar until they are pale.

2. Add the ground almonds, flour, baking powder and spices and mix.

3. Add the grated pumpkin and gently stir the mixture with a wooden spoon.

4. Pour the batter into a buttered and floured loaf tin, then bake at 180°C (350°F) for 50 minutes.

My witchcraft recipes and rituals

Index

191

Photo credits: